Selling to the Top

David Peoples'
Executive Selling Skills

Other Books by the Author

Presentations Plus (First Edition)

Presentations Plus (Second Edition)

Supercharge Your Selling:
60 Tips in 60 Minutes

Selling to the Top

David Peoples' Executive Selling Skills

David A. Peoples
Longboat Key, Florida

John Wiley & Sons, Inc.

New York   Chichester   Brisbane   Toronto   Singapore

Copyright © 1993 by David A. Peoples
Published by John Wiley & Sons, Inc.

All rights reserved. Published simultaneously in Canada.

Library of Congress Cataloging in Publication Data:
Peoples, David A., 1930–
    Selling to the top : David Peoples' executive selling skills /
David A. Peoples.
        p.   cm.
    ISBN 0-471-58104-6. -- ISBN 0-471-58105-4 (paper)
    1. Selling. 2. Selling--Key accounts.   I. Title.
HF5438.25.P448   1993
658.8'5--dc20   93-526
                                                       CIP

Printed in the United States of America

10 9 8 7 6 5 4 3 2 1

This book is dedicated to

Hervey Leigh Cunningham

Acknowledgments

There are not many subjects about which more has been written than selling. There is also no shortage of tapes, videos, seminars, and workshops on selling skills. My purpose is to focus the collective wisdom of outstanding and articulate thinkers on the subject of selling to the top. The first of these was Aristotle. Here are some of the others:

Anthony Alessandra   Dorothy Bolton
Robert Bolton   Thomas Bonoma
Dale Carnegie   Charles Garfield
Stephen Heiman   Wesley Johnson
Carl Jung   Michael LeBoeuf
Harvey Mackay   Mark McCormack
David Merrill   Robert Miller
Jim Pancero   Tom Peters
Michael Porter   Neil Rackham
Roger Reid   John Rockart
Robert Schaffer   Benson Shapiro
Tom Stanley   Frederick Webster
Roger Wenschlag   Larry Wilson
Yoram Wind   Zig Ziglar

The clip art is "Presentation Task Force," copyrighted by New Vision Technologies, Inc.

Contents

Chapter 7   What to Talk About?   117
(Answer: What's Important to Them)

- The concept of CSFs
- The best thing to do on the first call
- Questions to ask an executive
- The hardest thing in the world to do
- How to hear what the customer says
- Don't forget the key, the blocker,
  and the letter

Chapter 8   The Art of Persuasion   138
(Left Brain Selling; Right Brain Closing)

- Why people buy and how people buy
- How to win and how to lose
- Three things needed to persuade another
  person
- How to build trust
- Facts versus feelings
- Business reasons versus personal reasons

Chapter 9   Presenting the Answer 178
(How to Differentiate Yourself from Your Competitor)

- The breakthrough strategy
- The least-risk strategy
- Sell a business philosophy
- Conduct an ESS review
- Sell first choice for second place
- Don't talk across the desk

Selling to the Top

David Peoples'
Executive Selling Skills

Introduction

Selling
to the
Top

by
David
Peoples

What Is This Book All About?

This is a book about the benefits of calling at the top and the risk of calling at the bottom. It is about the wisdom of precision marketing to decision makers, not selling to the multitudes.

It is about understanding why people buy and knowing when to walk away. It is about getting around the blockers and getting to the boss.

It is about earning respect and trust by learning the client's business and understanding their problems.

It is about sizing up people in advance without ever having met them and modifying our behavior to be more compatible with our customers and clients.

It's knowing what to talk about and how to really hear what the client is saying. It is about solving business issues, not about selling features and functions. It's about feelings versus facts and personal reasons versus business reasons.

It is not about salesmanship but about building relationships and partnerships. This is a book that says, "If there's not much difference between your product or service and that of your competitor, then there better be a big difference in the way you deal with people."

It is about six strategies that will differentiate you from your competitor and make you a winner in the competitive marketplace.

It is about the required ingredients for success and the reality that only the persuaded can persuade.

How Did It Come to Be?

Something was wrong—bad wrong. For a quarter of a century, IBM had set the standards for growth, quality, and service in corporate America. It was consistently ranked as the best-managed and most-admired company in the country. Its major strength had always been its highly touted salesforce—said to be the best and the mightiest in the world.

But the glory days were fading fast. The 15 percent compound growth rate fell to 6 percent, then became flat. And then the unthinkable occurred; it actually declined in some markets.

IBM was not alone. Over much of corporate America, the story was the same or worse. What happened? What went wrong? The answers were complex and involved many issues. This book will focus on one—sales.

To get some answers, IBM commissioned a major study by an outside consulting firm. The study sought to discover two things:

1. The skills most critical for success in selling products or services that involved
   - Big money
   - Multiple decision makers
   - Long sales cycle
   - Top management approval
   - An ongoing relationship
2. IBM's level of performance of the most critical skills

Here is the ranking of the five skills that were found to be the most critical for success yet the lowest in level of performance:

1. Calling at the top
2. Consultative skills
3. Listening skills

tied {
4. Influencing skills
5. Questioning Skills
}

The study concluded that:

1. The skill that ranked the highest in importance, yet the lowest in performance, was calling on senior executives
   When salespeople were asked why they didn't call at a higher level, they gave two answers: "I don't know

what I would talk about" and "I don't feel comfortable calling at the top."

2. Dramatic changes were needed in the area of consulting skills, which are required to understand the customer's business issues and to develop solutions that address them.

3. Salespeople talk too much, listen too little, and don't know what questions to ask.

As a member of IBM's Advanced Business Institute, I was asked to develop an advanced sales training program for experienced salespeople that addressed these problems. It was an exciting project.

In the years since then, I have enhanced and built on many of those concepts, and I have seen them tested and proven in my workshops and seminars across a broad sampling of corporate America. This book is the end result.

It had become clear that the old selling ways were not working well, if they ever did. From the customer or client's point of view, the old techniques are so well understood that they are not only ineffective, they are actually offensive. Consider this, for example. If you make ten sales calls a week, that's 500 a year. How many selling techniques do you see? The answer is one—yours. But if you are the customer and you see two salespeople a day, that's also 500 a year. How many selling techniques does the customer see? The answer is many. Now, who would know more about sales techniques, you or the customer?

A review of the major sales training programs reveals that there's hardly a dime's worth of difference between them. Oh yes, there are different terminologies and methods of delivery as well as the use of different technologies. But there is an amazing consistency in steps and techniques.

We are trained to tell the story of the functions and features of our products or services as if we had the only game in town. But from the customer or client's point of view, all products and services are beginning to look alike, with only minor differences among them. To the customer, there is today a sameness to products, services, and salespeople. If you are pitching a quality product, with great service at a good price, what do you think your competitor is pitching? The same thing. Most customers in most industries believe there are multiple providers who can satisfy their requirements.

A major fallacy of most sales training is the idea that "one size fits all." Here are some examples of the mistakes this commonly leads to:

- Selling a million-dollar product the same way you would sell widgets
- Selling to an individual the same way you would sell to a committee
- Believing that one-call-close selling is the same as a one-year sell cycle
- Believing that you would sell to the president the same way you would sell to the purchasing agent
- Believing that the best way to handle objections is to memorize the answers to the 48 most common ones
- Believing that the best way to close is to practice 20 closing techniques like "the puppy dog close"

Times have changed. The old ways no longer work. The prospect is not the enemy, selling is not a contest, and the order is not a prize. The trick phrases or "gotcha" questions are recognized for what they are. The adversarial vendor relationship is being replaced by a recognition of the importance of a vendor partnership as outsourcing and interlocking arrangements have become the order of the day. Old-fashioned virtues of trust, integrity, and dependability have been born again.

Do I have all the answers? Have I captured some "killer bees" you can unleash on your competitor? Have I discovered a miracle drug you can use on your customer? Of course not. What I have are sound principles for building relationships and partnerships and how to solve customer problems by learning what they want and giving it to them.

If you would like more business with less effort by doing the right things the first time, then come along with me. Let's walk this road together. I believe you will find, as have others, that the man or woman who wants to do business with you can justify anything.

> David Peoples
> P.O. Box 8850
> Longboat Key, Florida 34228

1

Why Call at the Top?
(More Business—Less Effort)

If your product or your service involves

- Big money
- Multiple decision makers
- A long sales cycle
- Top management approval
- An ongoing relationship

then you're in the right place—and *this book is for you.*

We start with the single most important thing there is to know to be successful in this marketplace. (I know. I did it the wrong way for ten years.) Let me tell you my experience.

The lower I called in my accounts, the more comfortable I felt. The controller level was about as high as I would dare tread on the organization chart. I certainly wouldn't call at the top. Up there, I thought, they were all eight feet tall, had gone to Harvard, and had MBAs. (I later found out they ain't, they didn't, and they don't.)

I would usually find that before I could get any serious interest from controllers, they would want to see it, touch it, kick it, and analyze it. So I would go back to the ranch and arrange for a "demo." Comes the dawn and Demo day. It's a good show and a great story, but the controller says, "Our business is different. We would need to understand more specifically how it would work for us." So I would say, "Fine. Let me come out and do a study." Now I'm interviewing, analyzing, quantifying, and building the business case. I get back to the controller with the good news about reduced inventory, less people, and better customer service. Unfortunately, the customer's vision of the future is rarely as crystal clear as mine. They usually mumble those dreaded words, "We need it in writing." I hate to write proposals, but they come with the territory.

By the way, time has been marching on. I've got three or four weeks invested in this thing by now.

Finally, I'm giving my proposal presentation to the controller.

Let's assume that I've got a 50 percent chance of the controller saying yes. I take that branch—the controller says yes—so now the controller is going to sign the contract, right?

If you say wrong, you're right. Experienced salespeople know that there is no way a controller is going to sign a contract for a product or service that meets the criteria we described at the start of this chapter. So I've been messing around for weeks with someone who can't sign the contract. The controller has to get approval at the top; now I'm dependent on a controller to do my selling for me. But how good a salesperson do you think someone would be who has spent their life dotting debits and crossing credits?

For the decision maker at the top, this could well be one of the most important business decisions to be made all year. That being the case, do you think he or she might want to kick the tires and lift the hood? Absolutely. So here I am going through my steps a second time. Finally, I'm giving my proposal presentation to the decision maker. Let's assume I have a 50 percent chance of the decision maker saying yes. So where do I stand? I now have a 50 percent chance on top of the controller's 50 percent—a 25 percent chance of getting the business. But then the decision maker says those awful words (have you heard them?), "I owe it to the business to look at other vendors." Here I am with a 25 percent chance of getting the business, and now I get a competitive situation. Let's say we win 50 percent of the time in competitive situations. As we see in Figure 1.1, that means I now have a 12½ percent chance of getting the business, and I've got six weeks of my time invested in it. Surely there is a better way to money, fame, and glory than doing business that way. And sure enough there is. It's called Rule #1: Call at the Top.

More often than not, the person at the top is easiest to see (more about that later), and he or she will let you know up front whether or not you're wasting your time. This person can tell you the decision criteria, where you stand, and what you have to do to get the business. And they will be interested in

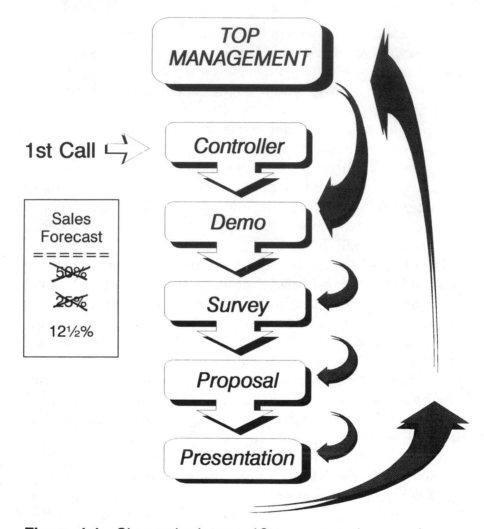

Figure 1.1   Six weeks later a 12½ percent chance of getting the business.

what you have to say if you know what to talk about (which we will learn in Chapter 7).

If you doubt the wisdom of Rule #1, let me ask you this question: Have you ever heard a person at the top say, "It's not in the budget"?

Figure 1.2   Rule #1—Call at the top.

The Worry Pyramid

Another way of looking at the wisdom of calling at the top is provided by Dr. Abraham Maslow's hierarchy of personal priorities, as shown in Figure 1.3. Here we see that human priorities from bottom to top are

1. Survival needs—"I want to be alive."
2. Security needs—"I want to be secure."
3. Social needs—"I want to be loved."
4. Sense of worth—"I want to be important."
5. Need for achievement—"I want to be great."

Figure 1.3 Hierarchy of personal priorities.

Figure 1.4 Hierarchy of business concerns.

If we overlay that concept on the corporate organizational structure, we get some insight into what people think about and worry about at different levels of the organization, as shown in Figure 1.4.

At the bottom of the organization, people worry about having a job (survival). When the job need is satisfied, they concern themselves with improving the quality of their job or getting a better job (security). When that need is satisfied, the focus shifts to projects and their departmental agenda (social needs). Only when we move to the fourth level do we find a serious interest in increasing sales, reducing cost, and improving production (sense of worth). And it is only at the very top that we find a concern about profit and the survival of the corporation.

The consequences of the worry pyramid cause dramatic differences in the relative value of marketing considerations at the top versus the bottom. Looking at the right-hand side of Figure 1.5, we see that the relative value of your product's *bells* and *whistles* increases as you go down the organizational chart but decreases as you go up the pyramid. The relative importance of the *dollars* (cost) is greater at the bottom than it is at the top. And the third item should get our attention if nothing else does.

WHY CALL AT THE TOP

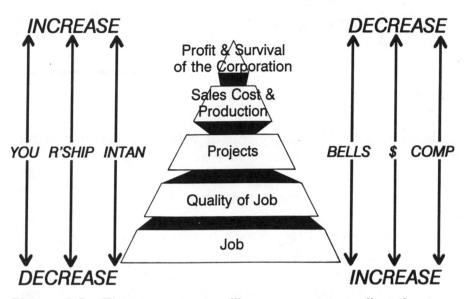

Figure 1.5   There are compelling reasons to call at the top.

There is almost always more *competition* at the bottom than there is at the top.

On the left side of Figure 1.5, we see that the value of *intangible* considerations increases at the top but decreases at the bottom. And as we know from Michael Porter's book *Competitive Strategies*, the vendor *relationship* is an important item to corporate success and survival. That truth is much better appreciated at the top than it is at the bottom. Finally, as the quarterback directing the relationship, we see that *you* can be perceived to have greater value to those at the top than those at the bottom.

In selling at the bottom, you are engaging in the classic struggle of value versus price in the competitive marketplace, as shown in Figure 1.6.

But at the top there is likely to be a more mature and realistic understanding of value versus price. It is more likely to be

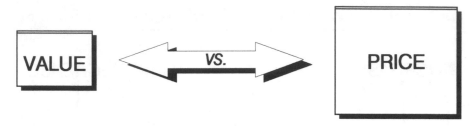

Figure 1.6   Selling at the bottom.

understood that the components of value are quality and service. So the relationship is more likely to be seen as

$$\text{Quality} + \text{Service} = \text{Price}$$

So a lower price probably means lower quality or less service, or both. In fact, for many (if not most) products, price is way down the list in the ranking of buying criteria.

This principle was described by John Ruskin over 100 years ago, as shown in Figure 1.7.

Zig Ziglar would describe it this way: When you add the benefits of quality, subtract the disappointments of cheapness, multiply the pleasure of buying something good, and divide the cost over a period of time, the arithmetic comes out in your favor.

In selling at the top we also have the opportunity to change the rules of the game and enhance the value by enlarging the decision considerations—and thereby change the balance between value and price, as shown in Figure 1.8.

Is this important? It sure is. For example, if a grizzly bear and a crocodile get into a fight, who will win? Answer: It depends on the ground rules. If the fight is on dry land, the bear wins. If the fight is in the water, the crocodile wins. If you can change the rules, you can win.

If you say, "But my product is a commodity. I don't have any exotic intangibles or other value to differentiate my product or service," listen to this quote from Ted Levitt at the Harvard Business School: "There is no such thing as a commodity. All

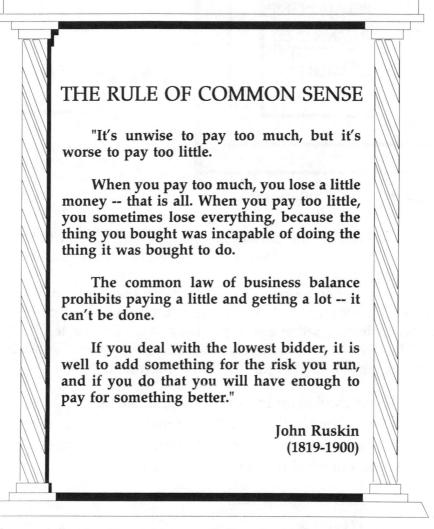

THE RULE OF COMMON SENSE

"It's unwise to pay too much, but it's worse to pay too little.

When you pay too much, you lose a little money -- that is all. When you pay too little, you sometimes lose everything, because the thing you bought was incapable of doing the thing it was bought to do.

The common law of business balance prohibits paying a little and getting a lot -- it can't be done.

If you deal with the lowest bidder, it is well to add something for the risk you run, and if you do that you will have enough to pay for something better."

John Ruskin
(1819-1900)

Figure 1.7 As true today as it was a century ago.

goods and services are differentiable." The proof comes from the chicken king, Frank Perdue. He says,"If you can differentiate a dead chicken, you can differentiate anything." (More about that in Chapter 9.)

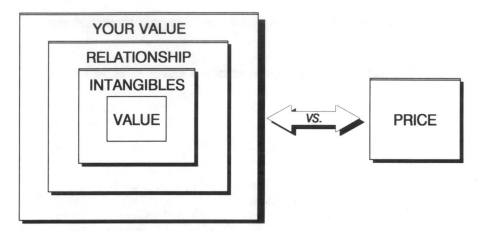

Figure 1.8   Selling at the top.

What kind of salesperson are you? Where do you fit in the wide world of selling? Take a look at Figure 1.9 and find where you would like to be.

Most salespeople say, "I want to be on the right." But when we ask customers, "Where on this scale would you place the salespeople you see every day?" they say, "On the left."

That leads us to Rule #2. Rule #2 is the second most important thing there is to know to be successful.

- If your marketing is based on added value
- If your strategy is based on differentiation
- If intangibles are important to your selling success
- If you tailor solutions to fit the customer

then you need to follow Rule #2:

CALL AT THE TOP

Guess what Rule #3 is?

What an Opportunity!!

Rarely in the course of business history has there been such an opportunity to outfox your competitor. Your competitor does

TYPES OF SALESPEOPLE

	PEDDLER	TRADITIONAL SALESPERSON	HIGH PERFORMANCE SALESPERSON	BUSINESS PARTNER/ CONSULTANT
CALLS ON	Purchasing Agent	User	Middle Management	Top Management
INTENT	To Be Considered	To Make Sales	Repeat Business	Account Control
FOCUS	Price	Features & Functions	Value Added	Cust. Goals & Objectives
RELATIONSHIP	Hit & Run	Casual	Win/Win	Trust & Confidence
STRATEGY	Price Performance	Application Solutions	Business Issues	Customer's Strategic Direction

Figure 1.9 Where do you fit in the wide world of selling?

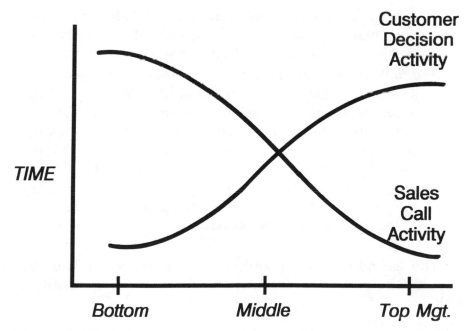

Figure 1.10 Where salespeople spend their time on the corporate pyramid.

not call at the top. Even at IBM (supposedly known for top management calls), only 5 percent of the salesperson's time is spent on top management calls, preparation, and follow-up. Take a look at Figure 1.10.

When salespeople are asked to explain the gross discrepancy between their call activity and where the decisions are made, they give the following reasons for not calling at the top:

1. *I have no value to offer at the top.* Answer: After you spend ½ day at the CIA (Chapter 5), you will not only be able to offer value—you may have some answers to his or her critical problems.
2. *I don't know what to talk about.* Answer: By the time you finish Chapter 7, you will not only know what to talk about—you will have a one-page script to follow.
3. *I need a heavy hitter (executive) to go with me.* Answer: Yes, you often do, and they are waiting on you. Just ask.
4. *I don't feel comfortable calling at the top.* Answer: We can't make the butterflies disappear, but by the time you finish this book, they will be flying in formation.
5. *I have no need to call at the top—business is good.* Answer: I promise you, this too will pass. We have all had accounts where an excellent relationship with a specific individual resulted in us getting all (or most) of the business. But believe me, one of two things will happen sooner or later. The day will come when that individual is fired, promoted, transferred, jumps ship, or dies. And their replacement has a love affair with brand X. That's called "kiss your career goodbye."

The second thing that can happen is unsportsmanlike conduct on the part of an executive of one of your competitors. Either out of desperation or enlightenment, they do the unthinkable. They call at the top in your account.

Here's what he or she will say: "We take a personal and vested interest in each of our customers. We assign one of our top executives as a direct liaison to your company. Our objective is to do more than we are paid to do and give better service than we are paid to give. Anytime you feel that we are not living up to that objective, you have an open line to our corporate office. I am the individual from the corporate office assigned to your company. We want to earn your business and deserve your confidence."

If that's your account, that's strong medicine. What if that account has been paying your company a zillion dollars a year for a period of years, and no executive from your company has ever called on their executive or even thanked them for the business? It's just a matter of time until you get the bad news phone call.

Over the years I have made a study of lost accounts, looking for common denominators to explain losses. They are hard to find. There is almost no limit to the creative imagination of salespeople in explaining and rationalizing a loss. I'm good at it myself. There is, however, one common denominator that appears with great consistency—the absence of an executive relationship.

Here is a true story that will tear your heart out. Following a major loss, a corporate executive arranged to call on the top decision maker. No one in his company had ever met or called on that individual during the sales effort. The executive said to the decision maker, "We would like to understand why you selected their product in light of the unique advantages of our product"—and he names them. To which the decision maker replied, "I wish somebody had told me about that 30 days ago." 'Nuff said.

There's More—30 Percent More

If you're like me, you know that you could do more (and do better) if you just had more time

Well, the only thing we all have the same amount of is time. But the biggest difference between us is how we use it. Consider,

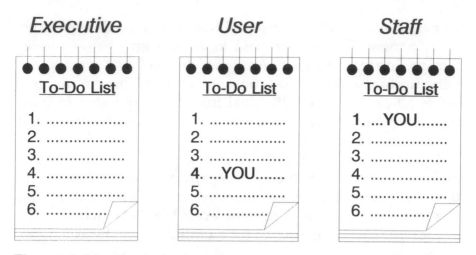

Figure 1.11 If we don't call at the top.

for example, the fact that over 30 percent of the time, the prospects end up not buying the product or service from anybody. If we could identify that 30 percent early in the game, then we could walk away and spend that time with another 30 percent who *are* going to buy. You can get that answer by calling at the top. The man or woman at the top can and will tell you flat out if they are serious or if you're wasting your time. More often than not, the people at the bottom either don't know or won't tell.

Realities of Corporate Life

Let's look at the effect of calling at the top versus not calling at the top by looking at the "to-do" lists of an executive, a user, and a staff person.

In scenario #1 (Figure 1.11) let's assume we do not call on the executive.

Clearly we do not make the executive's to-do list. Let's say that we call on the user. We get her attention and interest, and we make her to-do list—but not as a hot item, more likely near the bottom. Then the user turns to her staff and suggests that

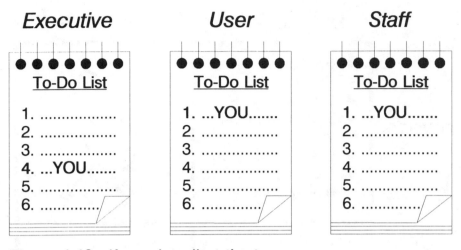

Figure 1.12 If we *do* call at the top.

they look into your business proposition. Because the staff works for the user, and because most people do what their boss tells them to do, your proposition goes to the top of the staff to-do list. That's good, but it's too bad that the staff is not the decision maker.

Now let's consider scenario #2 (Figure 1.12).

We do call on the executive. We get their interest and attention, and we make their to-do list—probably not at the top, but we're on the list. The executive turns to the user and suggests that she look into your business proposition. Again, because most people do what their boss tells them to do, we go to the top of the user's to-do list. The user makes the same suggestion to the staff, and again we're at the top of the staff list.

Would you rather have scenario #1 or scenario #2? Which is more likely to get you the business?

This raises two additional important questions. When I make the jump from calling on the user to calling on the executive, what happens to the dollar amount of the sign-off authority? Is it more likely to increase by 20 percent or by twentyfold?

And what happens to the decision timetable when I call on the executive? It can change from four months to four days or even four hours. That's called more business, less effort, less time.

Calling at Top   Not Calling at Top

	Calling at Top	Not Calling at Top
BENEFITS	• Easier sell • Faster sell • Less work • You have more value • Less competition • Can charge a higher price	
RISKS	**Make a fool of myself** - But not if you read Chapter 7	• Harder sell • Longer sell • More work • You have less value • More competition • Charge less

Figure 1.13 Why call at the top?

In Summary

The key reasons for calling or not calling at the top are summarized in Figure 1.13. There is one other reason for calling at the top. It has to do with the "left-brain problem," which we will get to shortly.

The Final Exam

If you've come this far, you're ready for the final exam. Fill in the blanks in Figure 1.14. If you score anything less than 100 percent, you need to schedule yourself for frontal lobotomy surgery and give this book to the guy or gal next door.

FINAL EXAM

1. In most companies the nicest person in the business is the _____ .

2. Contrary to popular myth, the easiest person to see is often the _____ .

3. The person least likely to have a hidden agenda is the _____ .

4. The future of the business is in the hands of the _____ .

5. The ultimate decision maker is the _____ .

6. The person who knows best what he or she needs to run the business is the _____ .

7. The only sure way to know if your strategy is aligned with the customer's strategy is to ask the _____ .

Figure 1.14 Passing grade is 100 percent.

2
How to Identify the Decision Makers
(Who Are the Players in the Game?)

A study by Wesley J. Johnson of Ohio State University and Thomas V. Bonoma of the Harvard Business School found that for major product purchases, there was an average of seven decision makers. For a major services purchase, there was an average of five decision makers. If you are the would-be seller or provider, you'd better know who's in a position to say yes. If you don't know where you're going, you'll never get there. And if you don't know who's buying, you're not likely to get the business.

We need to know the answers to the following questions:

- How many decision makers are there?
- Who are they?
- Who are the Influencers?
- Who is the Gatekeeper?
- Who is the DI (Dominant Influencer)?

The good news is that a lot of brain power has been focused on these questions over the years by some of the best folks in the business.

- Frederick Webster of the Amos Tuck School at Dartmouth and Yoram Wind of the University of Pennsylvania developed the "Buying Center Concept" in their book *Organizational Buying Behavior*.
- Thomas Bonoma and Benson Shapiro (both of Harvard), in their book *Segmenting the Industrial Market*, describe the different roles of the players encountered in purchase situations. They also discuss the importance of having an internal champion or advocate (coach).
- Robert Miller and Stephen Heiman, in their book *Strategic Selling*, simplified the role classifications.

We will take some ideas from each of these books and present a new composite picture of the buying center. Then we'll go one step further and develop the concept of the Dominant Influencer, or DI.

There are four types of decision makers who collectively make up the buying center for a particular decision.

The Economic Decision Maker

The characteristics of the Economic Decision Maker are summarized in Figure 2.1.

There is one—and only one—Economic Decision Maker for a specific sales situation. He or she has direct access to the money and is the only person who has the authority to release the money to pay for your product or service. The Economic Decision Maker also has veto power. Regardless of the wants and desires of the other players, the Economic Decision Maker can veto the entire project.

Identifying the Economic Decision Maker is not as easy as you might think. For example, do you think most people would guess too high or too low on the organization chart? The answer is too low. Most people guess at least one level (and often two levels or more) too low.

We can get some insight into the identity of the Economic Decision Maker by asking the question, "In my own company, what is the level at which this type of decision would be made?"

The best way to identify the Economic Decision Maker is to ask this question of everyone in the company you have contact with: "What is the decision process?" Listen carefully to the process that they describe, because they are telling you how to win. And listen carefully to the last step, which will identify the Economic Decision Maker. You can confirm this when you call on the suspected Economic Decision Maker by asking either of the following questions:

1. "Will you be making a recommendation or giving the final go ahead?"
2. "Who can veto this project?"

How your suspect answers these questions will tell you whether or not he or she is the Economic Decision Maker.

THE ECONOMIC DECISION MAKER

- Only One per Sale

- Has Direct Access to $$$

- Can Release the $$$

- Veto Power

- To Identify: Who Has Authority to Release $$$?

Figure 2.1 The Economic Decision Maker.

The time you spend doing detective work to identify the Economic Decision Maker is well spent. He or she is the central character of Rules #1, 2, and 3.

But here's the problem. Human nature being what it is, other people in the company will try to lead you to believe that they are the Economic Decision Maker. Sometimes you'll hear comments like this: "Mr. Johnson? Oh, he just rubber-stamps our recommendation." Lies, all lies.

The Users

The characteristics of the User are summarized in Figure 2.2.

As you would expect, there are often multiple Users. Their dominant characteristic is that your product or service will have a direct impact on their job performance. Not surprisingly, they make judgments about that impact.

If, for example, you are selling a product, their concerns might be in the areas of

- Reliability
- Training
- Downtime
- Ease of use
- Maintenance

To identify the Users, we ask this question: "Who will use or manage the use of this product or service?"

The Influencers

There can be other players in the game who have opinions and give advice. They are the Influencers, summarized in Figure 2.3. Their opinions and advice can be solicited or unsolicited. If they have unique knowledge about or experience with the product or service being considered, their opinion is often sought out.

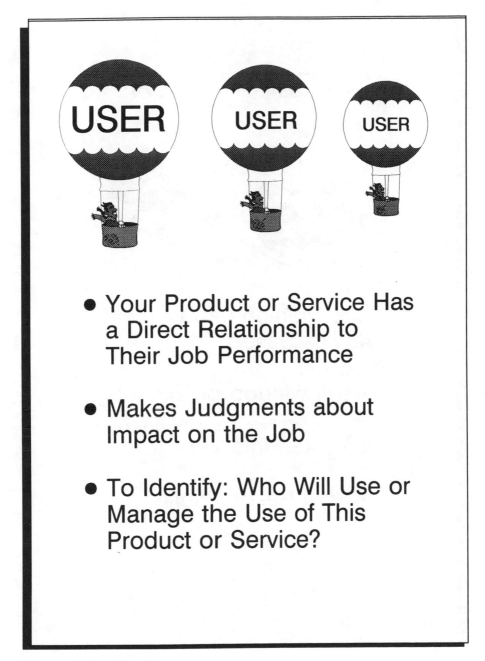

- Your Product or Service Has a Direct Relationship to Their Job Performance

- Makes Judgments about Impact on the Job

- To Identify: Who Will Use or Manage the Use of This Product or Service?

Figure 2 2   The User.

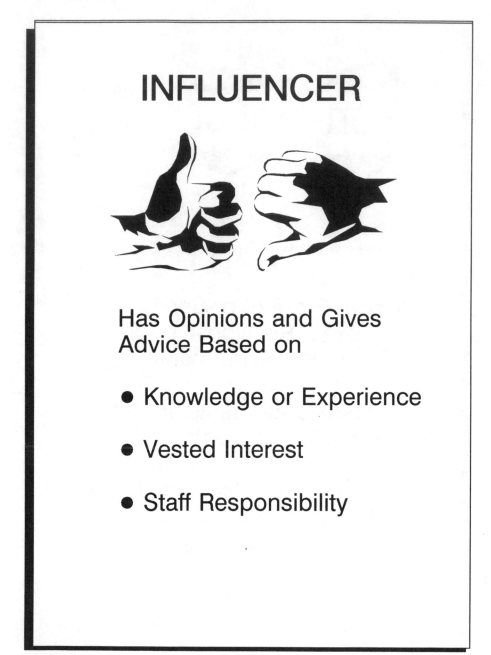

Figure 2.3   The Influencer.

Or, although not direct users, they may have a stake in the outcome of the decision. For example, the sales department may have a vested interest in the selection of a new electronic dispatch and data capturing system for the maintenance department. They would be interested in customer acceptance of and satisfaction with the new system. The data processing department may also have a vested interest in the new system if it involves new programming or interfacing with existing systems.

Influencers may also be staff people who view the subject under consideration to be within the scope of their staff responsibilities.

The Gatekeepers

The role of the Gatekeeper is summarized in Figure 2.4.

They decide which vendors or providers will be allowed to play in the game. They cannot make the "yes" decision, but they can exclude you from consideration.

Sometimes we lose and never know why. The truth may be that we were never a serious contender because a Gatekeeper excluded us from consideration.

A Gatekeeper may be

- A systems programmer who says, "Your computer response time does not meet the mandatory requirements of our RFP (Request For Proposal)."
- A staff person who says, "You have no experience in our industry."
- A controller who says, "The terms of your lease are not acceptable."
- A company lawyer who will not approve your contract.

Some companies have formalized and structured the role of Gatekeepers by creating an "approved vendor list."

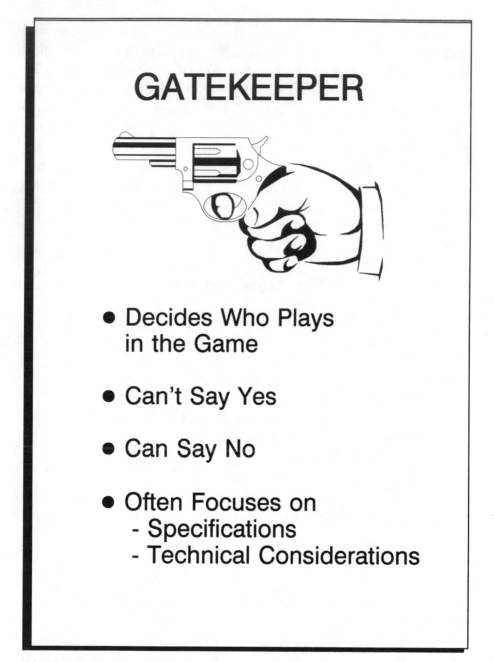

Figure 2.4 The Gatekeeper.

The Coach

Our final player in the game is the Coach, summarized in Figure 2.5. In some ways the Coach is the most important player. If you have no Coach, you are almost literally selling in the dark.

COACH

- **Your Guide in This Sale**

- **Wants You to Win**

- **Has Credibility within the Company**

- **Has Confidence in You**

Figure 2.5 The Coach.

Experienced salespeople refer to their Coach as their "inside salesman," and his or her role is to guide you in this sale. High performance salespeople identify, develop, and cultivate Coaches. A Coach is often a person who has had a successful (win/win) experience with you. A good Coach can tell you the names of other players in the buying center for this particular sale.

We would normally think of the Coach as an employee of the customer or client, but they can be in other places:

- An industry consultant
- A CPA
- An ex-employee
- Within your own company—for example, the former sales rep on the account

Of course, the ideal situation would be one where the Economic Decision Maker is also the Coach. Next best would be if a User or Influencer is also your Coach. And if you have more than one Coach for this sales situation, so much the better.

The players in the buying center who have a vote (though not an equal vote) are summarized in Figure 2.6.

Now comes the acid test. Think of a major account situation you are currently involved in where the winner has not yet been decided. Fill in the names of the players in Figure 2.7.

If you do not know or aren't sure, don't guess. Too much is at stake. Instead, put a question mark in the name box. If you do not know or aren't sure you've got them all, put a question mark in the box. If you aren't sure whether or not you have a Coach, the answer is you don't. Put a question mark in the Coach box.

THE BUYING CENTER

Figure 2.6 A buying center.

In my seminars, when I ask for a show of hands, 80 percent of the attendees have one or more question marks. Guess which player has the most questions marks. You got it—the Economic Decision Maker, the most important name on the page. It's hard

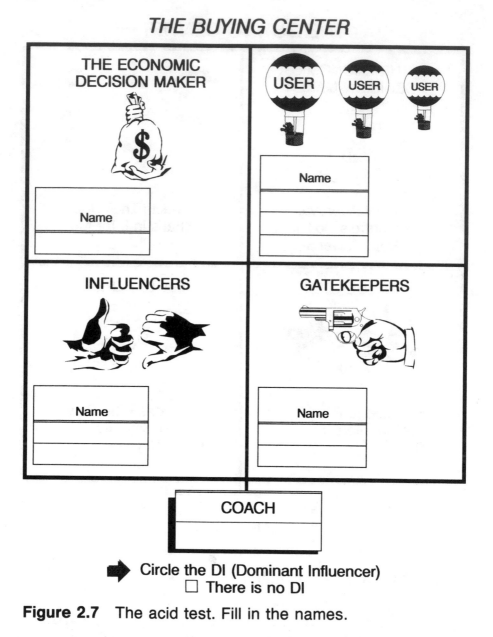

Figure 2.7   The acid test. Fill in the names.

to execute Rules #1, 2, and 3 if you don't know the name of the Economic Decision Maker.

A single question can be of immense help in identifying the decision makers. The question to ask of each of your contacts is "Who else is going to be involved in this decision?" Usually a clear pattern will emerge. So if you have question marks, it's time to get on the phone or get in your car and get some answers. Remember, companies don't buy—people do.

The DI (Dominant Influencer)

Knowing the names in the buying center is not enough. They are not all equal, nor do they have an equal vote. Corporate decision making is not a democratic process. The organization chart can be grossly misleading in terms of the power and influence involved in a particular decision.

Just ask yourself the following questions:

- Do you listen up and pay more attention when certain people talk?
- Do you respect the opinion and judgment of some more than others?
- Have you ever heard anybody say, "What does _____ think?"

Think of some of the meetings you have attended in your own company (or the PTA) that involved making a decision on a particular subject. Sometimes after literally hours of discussing the pros and cons of various alternatives, we seem to be getting nowhere. Finally, someone (the Economic Decision Maker) turns to Joan (who has been quiet during most of the discussion) and asks, "Joan, what do you think?"

Suddenly we hear articulated a crystal clear logic that puts the pros and cons in perspective: the relative importance of various considerations becomes clear. Suddenly "the right thing" appears to be obvious. Heads begin to nod as people say, "Joan is right." Suddenly the decision is made. What we have witnessed is the DI (Dominant Influencer) in action.

If your product or services were being discussed in that meeting, you would get the business if you had sold just one person—Joan.

Clearly, we can save a lot of time, be more effective, and enhance our odds if we can identify and market to the DI.

So how do we identify the DI? They come in two flavors:

1. The authority or recognized expert on the subject under consideration
2. A trusted advisor and confidant of the Economic Decision Maker

The authority or expert DIs are easily identified because they are clearly visible and their expertise is acknowledged by the other players. Consider, for example, the DI role of the company pilot in the selection of a new company plane.

What puts these people in the role of DI is that they are the only (or one of a very few) experts on this subject in their companies, and their superior knowledge or experience is respected by the other decision makers.

This would be in contrast, for example, to computer experts within a company, of whom there may be many with different views and none clearly recognized as superior to the others. So in the field of computers, the DI may be a trusted advisor who may or may not be a computer heavyweight.

The trusted advisor type of DI is more difficult to identify. They are neither the most visible nor the most talkative. And they are often hidden in the maze of the organization chart. But even the most powerful Economic Decision Makers are influenced by the DI, who has a track record of good advice and good results. These are people who, by virtue of their judgment and performance, have earned the confidence and respect of the Economic Decision Maker.

Here are some of their characteristics:

- When they speak, others listen
- Rarely surprised by events (they have inside information)
- Understand company goals, objectives, and strategy
- Results-oriented
- High level of personal integrity
- Calculated risk-taker
- Well-organized
- Always prepared
- Sought out for advice and opinion
- Copied on internal correspondence that pertains to a pending purchase
- Has a sense of priorities
- Good listener

Of course, nobody walks around with those labels on his or her forehead, and we can't go around interrogating people. So we need a practical (and hopefully, simple) way to identify this type of DI. We can do that by asking our Coach four questions:

1. When the Economic Decision Maker was promoted to his or her present position, who was brought along from his or her previous job?
2. Whom does the Economic Decision Maker socialize with, carpool with, lunch with, or exercise with?
3. Who frequently attends the Economic Decision Maker's meetings?
4. Who has received a recent promotion that required the approval of the Economic Decision Maker?

If you get a hit on any of the four questions, you have a good suspect. Two or more hits and you probably have your answer.

The Dominant Influencer can be

1. One of the Users
2. One of the Influencers
3. A Gatekeeper

Here's the critical question. Of all the players in the buying center, is there one whose opinion and judgment the Economic Decision Maker respects more than others'? Or we can pose the question another way. If the Economic Decision Maker could ask the opinion of just one person, whom would they ask?

If you have trouble identifying the DI, it may be because there is no Dominant Influencer for this sales situation. Be especially skeptical of those who talk loud and often. They would like for you to think that they are the Dominant Influencers—but they rarely are.

Our next step is to circle the name of the DI on the buying center worksheet (Figure 2.7), or check the box indicating that there is no DI.

Identifying the players in the buying center is time well spent because it guarantees that you will avoid the two greatest sins of selling:

1. Making a perfect presentation to someone who has no voice in the decision.
2. Having no contact and no communication with the person who has the strongest voice in the decision.

Opportunity Knocking

If your customer or client experiences one of the following:

- Merger
- Consolidation
- Reorganization
- or New Management

you're looking at a time of great opportunity. Here's three reasons why:

1. Your competition will be confused and slow to understand the new players. They will tend to continue with their old contacts who may be out of the loop and out of the game.
2. You have a structure, a methodology, and the right questions that will allow you to quickly identify the new players in the buying center.
3. The new players in the buying center will be receptive to new ideas and new ways. They are often brought in because the old ways weren't working. You will never have a more receptive audience. They have no logical or emotional ties to the old ways or the old team. They will want to run the railroad a new way, so it's a great opportunity for you to get on board the train.

3
Am I Going to Win or Lose?
(How to Get the Answer in Advance)

Wouldn't it be nice to know in advance whether you are going to win or lose? How much more productive we could be if we could concentrate on surefire situations and walk away from lost causes. In this chapter we will discuss some techniques for getting that answer.

We'll start with a summary of buyer attitudes from the book *Strategic Selling* by Robert Miller and Stephen Heiman. We will then enhance those concepts by presenting additional approaches to the question "Will I win?" With this as a foundation, we'll then describe four winning strategies to get more business with less effort by doing the right things.

From the previous chapter we now have the names of all the decision makers in the buying center, and we have identified the DI (Dominant Influencer). Our next step is to answer this question: "Are they going to end up buying something from somebody?" This is important because, as we said in the first chapter, over 30 percent of the time the prospect or client ends up not doing business with anybody. If we can identify those who comprise that wasted 30 percent in advance, we will have plenty of time to do the right things at accounts that are going to buy.

When the time comes for each decision maker to vote on whether or not to do business with somebody, will they vote yes or no?

Here's the principle. *People will buy when there is a discrepancy between their perception of where they are and their opinion of where they should be.* Simply put, no discrepancy = no sale.

Whatever our product or service, there are four possible states of mind for each decision maker.

1. *Growth* (Figure 3.1). In the mind of this decision maker, there is a significant discrepancy between his perception of where he is and his opinion of where he should be in the area under consideration, which could be customer service, inventory control, production equipment, professional services, or whatever. This decision maker perceives that he has "outgrown" his old toys or old ways.

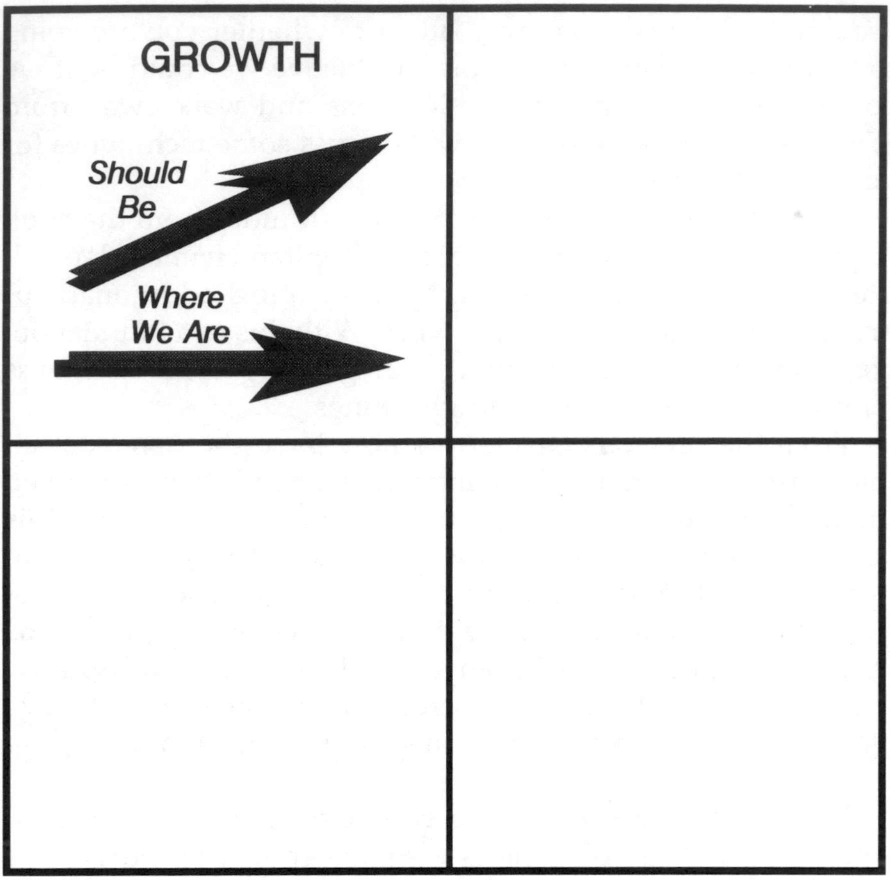

Figure 3.1   The Growth state of mind is ready to buy.

Whatever the product or service, this decision maker is ready to say yes to somebody. You will hear him say things like:

"We need more . . . "

"We need better . . . "

"We need faster . . . "

2. *Trouble.* (Figure 3.2). In this decision maker's mind things were in good shape until something happened and things went downhill fast. You will hear her say things like:

"We're hurting."

"It's a crisis."

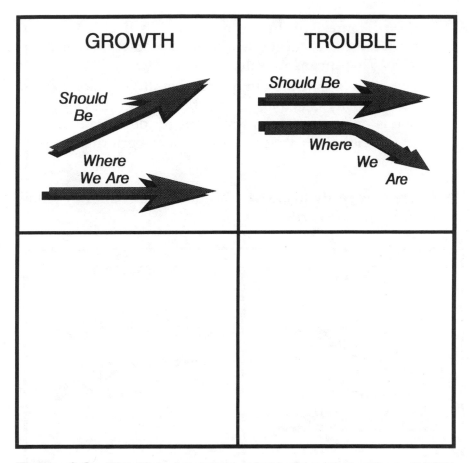

Figure 3.2 The Trouble state of mind wants action—FAST.

"We need to fix it and get back to normal."

"We need relief."

The trouble situation could even be the result of good news. For example, a sudden 30 percent increase in orders has resulted in a deterioration of customer service. This decision maker is *not* impressed with bells and whistles, new technology, or the lowest price. She *is* interested in the fastest solution that's proven, reliable, and low risk. It's the alligators that have her attention, not the draining of the swamp.

3. *Even* (Figure 3.3). In the mind of this decision maker, everything is copacetic. There is no problem, no discrepancy. That means no sale.
4. *Too Good* (Figure 3.4). In the mind of this decision maker, the company is actually doing better than they need to. She is either complacent and out of touch with reality, or else her goals are so low that poor performance isn't obvious.

We are now ready to answer this question: "Are they going to buy from somebody?"

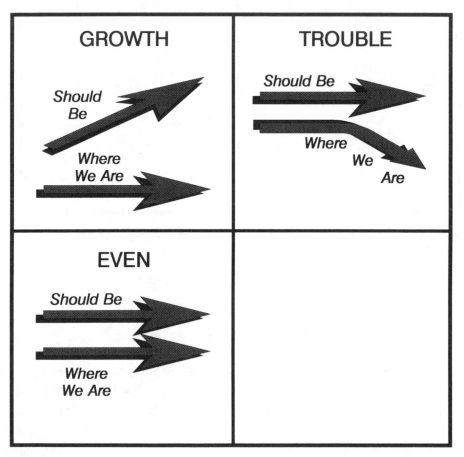

Figure 3.3 Even state of mind: no discrepancy—no sale.

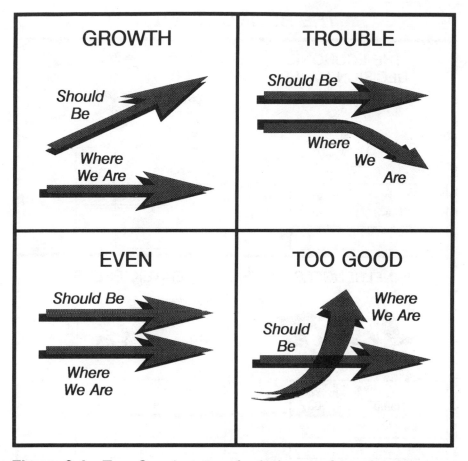

Figure 3.4 Too Good state of mind: out of touch with reality.

Referring to our Decision Makers' Worksheet (Figure 3.5), we want to fill in the "Will Buy" box with a yes or no. If their state of mind is Growth or Trouble, the answer is "Yes—they are going to do business with somebody." If, on the other hand, their state of mind is Even or Too Good, then the answer is no.

If you don't know or aren't sure, put a question mark in the box and remind yourself to make some sales calls or talk to your Coach and get some answers.

Finally we come to the big question:

THE BUYING CENTER

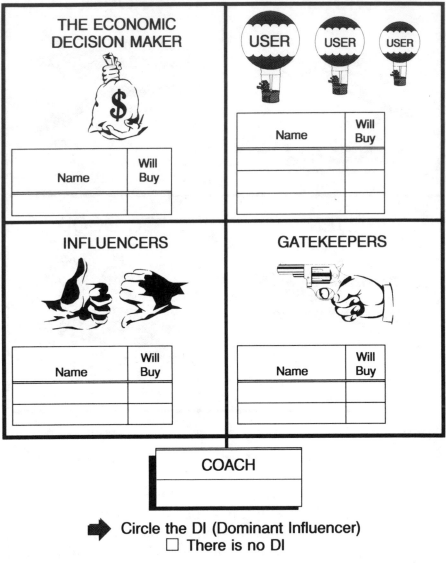

Circle the DI (Dominant Influencer)
☐ There is no DI

Figure 3.5   Fill in the "Will Buy" box with Yes, No, or ?

Are They Going to Buy from Me?

We will present three different techniques for getting the answer to this question. Take your pick. Or, if this is a big decision with a lot at stake, use all three.

The first technique is to ask ourselves the following question about each decision maker: "What is their attitude right now towards our business proposition?" Pick an answer on a scale from +5 to −5.

+5 Enthusiastic
+4 Strong support } YES
+3 Support

+2 Interested
+1 Will go along
−1 Won't resist } ?
−2 Uninterested

−3 Mildly negative
−4 Strong for competition } NO
−5 Antagonistic

If their attitude is a +3, +4, or +5, then the answer for that decision maker is YES—they will buy from you.

Clearly, if their attitude is a −3, −4, or −5, the answer is NO—they will not buy from you.

If their attitude is a +1, +2, −1, or −2, the answer is a question mark. If you don't know their attitude, the answer is also question mark.

Let's now turn to Figure 3.6 and fill in the "From Me" box with a yes, no, or ? for each decision maker.

A second approach to finding out if you are going to win or lose is shown in Figure 3.7.

On the left we prioritized the customer's buying criteria on a scale from crucial (at the top) to incidental (at the bottom).

THE BUYING CENTER

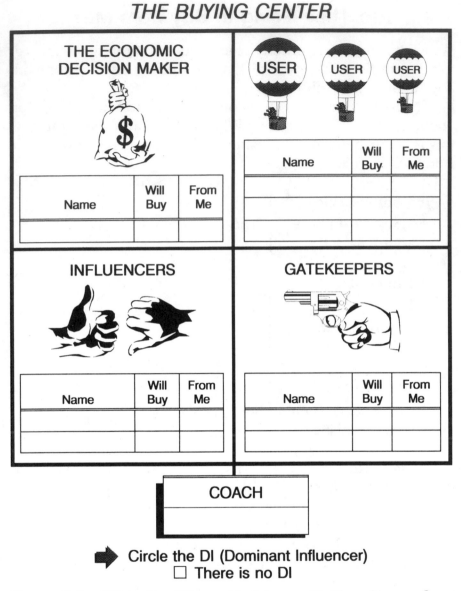

Circle the DI (Dominant Influencer)
☐ There is no DI

Figure 3.6 Fill in the ''From Me'' box with Yes, No, or ?

Am I Going to Win or Lose?

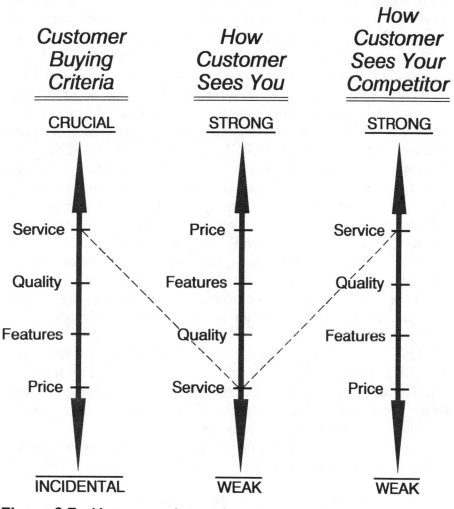

Figure 3.7   You are going to lose.

On the center scale we position our strengths and weaknesses as perceived by the customer.

Then on the right we position our competitor's strengths and weaknesses.

The "V" formed by the dotted line shows the gross incompatibility between what's important to the customer and their view of us compared to our competitor. So even though we have the lowest price and the best features, we are probably going to lose. The customer wants service and quality. The "V" is not for victory; it's a funnel that is sending us down the tubes.

To get the information to construct the chart, ask the DI.

When you get an RFP (Request for Proposal or Price) that you didn't know was coming, you have probably already lost. Here's why. The RFP will describe the requirements or specifications—spell that BUYING CRITERIA. In arriving at the buying criteria, the people who wrote the RFP had to have some base of reference. That is, they had to have some understanding of what's available in the marketplace. If they didn't get that information from you, then they got it from one of your competitors. That means the vendor selection is already biased in the competitor's favor because the product or service characteristics of the competition are reflected in the RFP.

If the time and effort to respond to this RFP are significant, you should seriously consider a "walk away" strategy. More about that in a minute.

The third technique to get some insight into whether you are going to win or lose has to do with how much weight you have on three scales called Logos (logic), Pathos (emotion), and Ethos (trust). A detailed discussion of these is coming up in Chapter 8, "The Art of Persuasion."

So there we have it on one page—a snapshot of where we stand with the answers to the following questions:

- How many decision makers are there?
- What are their names?
- Are they going to buy from somebody?
- Are they going to buy from me?
- Who is the DI (Dominant Influencer)?

There's just one problem. If you're like most of the people in my seminars, you have three or more question marks—worse, you probably have *more* question marks for the most important person on the page (the Economic Decision Maker) than for any other person.

But let me tell you the good news. You know exactly what you don't know. Your competitor doesn't. You can get the answers to the question marks. Your competition doesn't even know what questions to ask. Here's the bottom line: The more information and the more knowledge you have, the more likely you are to win.

And here's more good news. It's early in the game to talk about strategy, because some important pieces of the puzzle are yet to come. But just in case you lose your way or lose the book, here in Figure 3.8 are four winning strategies you can use today.

The Fast-Track Strategy

If you want the most business with the least effort in the shortest time, this is for you. The key to this strategy is to call on the Economic Decision Maker with two messages:

1. "We would like the opportunity to make a formal presentation to you and the other people involved in this decision to tell our story."
2. "The objective of the presentation is to give you *all* the information you need to make a *final* decision on our product or service for your business."

Your purpose with this strategy is to use a formal presentation as a catalyst to get all the players in the buying center together and to tell your story one time professionally rather than many times unprofessionally. An Economic Decision Maker would have the authority to call that kind of meeting. The not-so-subtle objective of the second message is to convey your expectation of a decision at the end of the presentation. This strategy is fast, simple, and, would you believe, rare. The key to its success lies in the effectiveness of your presentation

4 WINNING STRATEGIES

1. Fast-Track

2. Focused

3. Precision Marketing

4. Walk-Away

Figure 3.8   Tailor your strategy to your situation.

(more about that later). Suffice it to say for now that it's a one-time job to put together a professional presentation that tells the story of your product, your service, your support, and your people. With minor modification that same presentation can be used over and over. That's the kind of leverage that will produce more business with less effort. If you're not interested for yourself, think of your children. Don't they deserve wealthy parents?

The Focused Strategy

The Fast-Track Strategy is not appropriate for every situation, nor can you always get all the players together.

That leads us to the Focused Strategy. It gets its name because it focuses all your marketing activities on the two most important people in the buying center—The Economic Decision Maker and the DI (Dominant Influencer). If you can sell these two people, five will get you ten that you will get the business. And it sure takes a lot less time than trying to sell all seven players involved in the average major decision.

The Precision Marketing Strategy

If it's a really big deal, if the stakes are high and the reward is great, then you can't afford the risks that are inherent in the shortcuts of the Fast-Track or Focused Strategy. Moreover, there is not always a DI (Dominant Influencer), and that automatically excludes the Focused Strategy.

The Precision Marketing Strategy requires that you identify all the players and make the following informed judgments about each player:

1. Are they going to buy from somebody?
2. Are they going to buy from *me*?

The design of the Buying Center Worksheet in Figure 3.6 gives you the answers to all of the above. It identifies specifically where you have question marks or unfavorable answers. Your marketing efforts can now be directed by means of a Precision Marketing Strategy to the problem areas. The key to this strategy is unequal treatment of the players in the buying center. You should focus not on the positive but on the problems.

Your goal is not necessarily to win the problem players over (which is often impossible) but to neutralize them. If we can just accomplish that, then the positive votes of the other players will carry the day.

The Walk-Away Strategy

Sometimes the winningest strategy of all is to walk away. In fact, walking away can often improve your effectiveness by 100 percent.

I know it sounds crazy, but stay with me a couple of minutes. First, let's talk about sales forecasting.

If there is anything salespeople are worse at than forecasting, I don't know what it is. I think I was one of the worst offenders. Business never seemed to close when I thought it would. The realities of the buying center rarely matched my optimism. Looking back, I can see that I was always forecasting the answer to the "From Me" question. If I felt there was an 80 percent chance of them buying from me rather than my competitor, then I would forecast the business at 80 percent . What I never took into consideration was the "Will Buy" question. To continue the example, if there was only a 50 percent chance of them buying *something from somebody*, then my odds of getting the business were 40 percent (50% × 80%), *not* 80 percent.

So the first step in the Walk-Away Strategy is to breathe realism into your forecast. Now let's look at two ways to run a territory. In Figure 3.9, I have three account situations. Let's assume that each of the three involves the same amount of money and the same margin. My true forecast for each of the three is 40 percent, and I invest one-third of my time in each of the three situations. When the game is over and the smoke

Account Situations	Forecast	Time Invested	Number That I Will Win
#1	40%	1/3	
#2	40%	1/3	} 0 to 1
#3	40%	1/3	

Figure 3.9 One way to run your railroad.

Account Situations	Forecast	Time Invested	Number That I Will Win
#1	60%	1/2	
#2	60%	1/2	} 1 to 2
#3	0%	0	(a 100% increase)

Figure 3.10 Another way to run your railroad.

has cleared, how many of the three will I get? Most people agree that I will probably get somewhere between zero and one.

Now let's look at Figure 3.10. I have the same three situations. But look at the third column. Instead of spending one-third of my time on situation #1, I am going to spend one-half of my time. When I do that, it improves my forecast from 40 percent to 60 percent. How I use that additional time to improve the forecast is coming up. For now, please keep the faith.

I do the same thing for situation #2—spend one-half of my time and improve my forecast to 60 percent. But I walk away from situation #3. I spend no time and have a forecast of 0 percent for situation #3. Now I ask, how many am I going to close? This time most people agree that I will close somewhere between one and two, or a 100 percent increase.

So if you would like to double your pleasure, use the Walk-Away Strategy.

How do you know when to walk away? Check your Buying Center Worksheet. Do you have big question marks and many negative answers? Focus especially on the Economic Decision Maker and the DI. If the news is bad—walk away. You cannot be all things to all people. As we discussed earlier, you should also consider the Walk-Away Strategy when you receive an RFP you didn't know was coming. Use the time you save to improve your odds in better situations.

4

How to Meet Mr./Ms. Big

(It's Easier Than You Think)

Mr. or Ms. Big is the Economic Decision Maker for a specific sales situation. He or she is the most important person in the Buying Center and deserves our first and highest consideration.

We will greatly enhance our chances of getting the business if we have a meaningful call on the person who grants the final approval.

But how do you get an appointment with Mr./Ms. Big?

Because most people expect a complex or mysterious answer, let me tell you what I do during seminars to answer that question. I say, "I need a $20 bill. Would someone let me have a $20 bill?" No sooner are the words out of my mouth than hands are in the air with $20 bills. I then say, "The best way to get an appointment with Mr./Ms. Big is the same way I got this $20 bill—*JUST ASK.*"

In over 30 years as a salesman, sales manager, branch manager, and industry manager, I have never encountered a situation where I could not get an audience with the person at the top if I had a valid reason and was able to articulate that reason in a way that was of interest to him or her. I assure you, the probability of success should erase your fear of rejection.

Contrary to what you might think, the Economic Decision Maker is often the easiest person to see. *JUST ASK.* And, by the way, the higher up the organization you go, the nicer they are. Now, you don't get off scot-free. You have to be prepared to answer these three questions:

1. Who from your company is going to be at the meeting?
2. What is the purpose of the meeting?
3. How long will it take?

If you say, "But I don't know what I would say to a person at that level," have no fear. When we finish Chapter 7, we will not only know what to talk about but will also have a shorthand script to follow.

It will greatly facilitate matters if you follow the unspoken rules of protocol when calling on executives. Have someone from your company of the same rank and horsepower as the

Economic Decision Maker go with you on the first call. The bigger they are, the more critical this is. You may be able to go it alone on follow-up calls, but take a heavy hitter with you on the first call. You'll be glad you did. It's the best way to find an open door and a receptive mind.

Here are three direct approaches to the mechanics of asking for an appointment:

1. March right up to his or her secretary with the answers to the three questions (who, what, and how long) and ask for an appointment.
2. Write him or her a letter with the answers to the three questions. Figure 4.1 is an example of such a letter. You will see this letter again in Chapter 9 because it also embodies a sales strategy that could be important to you.
3. Have your executive's secretary call their secretary with the answers to the three questions and have them schedule a date.

If you have trouble articulating a purpose for the call, try something like this: " I'd like to learn more about your business and your objectives and to share some information about our expertise in your industry so that you can determine if there are areas in which we could mutually benefit."

But I'm Locked In at a Lower Level

I would observe that the biggest problem with calling at the top is not getting an appointment but the fear of trying caused by a real or imagined perception of being locked in at a lower level. When I ask for a show of hands, an amazing 75 percent confess to being locked in downstairs. That person who has you locked in is called a blocker.

Let's consider the worst-case situation, where the blocker has conveyed the message that going over his or her head will mean getting your throat cut. In that kind of situation, I would

Dear Mr./Ms. Executive:

We value our partnership with ___(customer or client name)___ .
It is our objective to provide value and solutions to your
business issues. In doing so we assume total accountability for
our products, our service, and our support. In order that we
may evaluate our effectiveness, it is our practice to meet with
our key customers (clients) for an Executive Service and
Support Review.

This is not a sales presentation. Its purpose is to

* Say "Thank you" for your business
* Review a summary of our activities with your
  company over the past year and the results
  achieved
* Invite your feedback on the quality and value of
  our products (or service or support)
* Listen to your suggestions as to how we might
  serve you better
* Present our planned activities for the coming year
  and confirm that they are aligned with your
  business goals and your priorities

It has been our experience that these reviews are mutually
beneficial in retaining and enhancing both of our competitive
positions in the marketplace.

Mr./Ms. ___(executive from your company)___ , our ___(title)___ ,
and I are looking forward to meeting you. You might wish to
invite other members of your management team to join us. We
expect that the meeting would last approximately 30 minutes.

I will call you on ___(date)___ to arrange for a convenient date.

Sincerely, etc.

Figure 4.1 This letter can get you an appointment at the top.

suggest that it's just a matter of time until you lose the business anyway. The values and priorities in decision making at a lower level will not always be in your favor.

If your value-added and your intangibles are not appreciated at a lower level and if there is no communication of that value to more receptive minds, you will be cutting your own throat by being forced to sell into the strength of your competitor. And if that doesn't get you, the unchivalrous conduct of calling at the top by one of your competitors will. Some competitors won't know that they are supposed to be locked in at a lower level.

And you run the risk of the "gangrene effect." First you lose a toe, then you lose a foot, then a leg. The next thing you know, it's gotten you by the throat. A good example of this is the computer business where first you lose the maintenance contract and then you lose the disk drives. Shortly thereafter you lose the PCs, and the next thing you know, you've lost the mainframe business. As I said in Chapter 1, a common denominator of lost accounts is the absence of an executive relationship.

So if you feel locked in, here in Figure 4.2 are ten keys to the lock:

1. *White Hat versus Black Hat.* This one is almost as old as recorded history. Your company executive plays the bad guy (Black Hat) by contacting the customer executive for an appointment. You will seem as innocent as the driven snow (White Hat) because you obviously cannot control the behavior of your executives.

2. *Show Them How They Will Win.* This is the most effective and longest-lasting solution. If the blocker believes that it is in his or her best interest for you to call upstairs, he or she will not only support you, but may also actually encourage you to call at the top.

   In a study of IBM's largest customers, the following question was asked: "How would you feel if the IBM salesperson went over your head and called above you?" Their surprising answer was: "It's not a problem if I have

Figure 4.2   How to unlock a locked situation.

trust and confidence in the salesperson. It's a big problem if I don't have trust and confidence in the salesperson." We will talk later about the specifics of building trust and confidence. For now let's just say that an important element is being predictable. Can the customer at a lower level predict what you will say at a higher level? They can if you tell them. You can lay the groundwork by asking your lower-level contact questions like these: "Do the folks upstairs know what a great job you did in installing X? Do they know the conversion was completed in half the time of the industry average? Do they know what a great team you have built? It may not be appropriate for you to tell them, but I can. What if we plan a joint call to brief them on our recommendations for the Zider Zee project. That would also give me the opportunity to tell your story for you."

Well, how often does the lower level have the opportunity for their superboss to hear how great they are? We are all human, and the deepest principle in human nature is the desire to be appreciated. Wouldn't you like to have a press agent? If I am the customer, it becomes very clear to me that it's in my best interest for you to call upstairs. I will win. Moreover, it may be that your lower-level person has never even been in the office of Mr./Ms. Big, let alone participated in a presentation to them. That's a big deal.

Sometimes, however, it's not appropriate in your customer's culture for Mr. Little to call on Ms. Big. In that environment you can prepare and rehearse to Mr. Little what you would present to Ms. Big.

That brings us to a cardinal rule of building relationships and turning blockers into buddies. Anytime you make an executive call, do not leave the building without meeting with the ex-blocker to give them a detailed briefing of the call with special emphasis on the comments and reactions of the executive. That's an ingredient of the glue that builds relationships and cultivates coaches.

3. *You Have Something They Need.* A variation of the technique we just described is to demonstrate to the blocker that you have something the Economic Decision Maker needs.

These people are paid six or seven figures for their ability to plan ahead, to forecast the future, and to ensure that they profit from future conditions. Their success is predicated on the clarity of their crystal ball. They need information, new ideas, fresh concepts—anything that will help them reach a profitable destination safely and on time. If you do your homework as described in Chapter 5 ("1/2 Day at the CIA"), if you truly understand their business, you may well have something the Economic Decision Maker needs. You may have thoughts and ideas on pending legislation, how to differentiate their product, improve customer service, or exploit the biggest weakness of their largest competitor. Or here's one that always gets their interest and attention: an overview of what's going on in their industry in your area of expertise. Only you can deliver that presentation.

4. *Buy a Piece of the Rock.* Be a stockholder in their company. That changes you from a vendor to an owner of the business. You will be amazed at the difference in attitude toward you when they find out you are a stockholder. That makes you one of them. And you don't have to buy a thousand shares; ten will do. Just make the list—the stockholders' list, that is. Then be sure you attend the main event, which is the annual stockholders' meeting. If it's a hometown company, the stockholders' meeting will be in River City, not New York City. And there won't be thousands of people there, just a few hundred. Be sure you sit in the front row.

Let me tell you a story. One of my customers was the home office of an insurance company. The president was Mr. John Robinson. No one from my company had ever met him. I was getting nowhere with the folks downstairs, so I bought ten shares of stock (all I could afford). In due course I got the invitation to the annual stockholders' meeting to be held at a local hotel.

There were only a couple hundred people there. And they had a receiving line made up of the officers of the company. At the end of the line was Mr. Robinson. (I knew it was him because they had his portrait hanging in the lobby of the home office.) As I progressed down the receiving line, I noticed that the attendees' names were being passed down the line. Because I knew the controller in the receiving line, I was sure my name was among them. And sure enough, when I stood in front of Mr. Robinson, he said, "I believe you're our IBM man." I replied, "Yes I am, Mr. Robinson." He said, "Thank you so much for coming to our meeting. Come up and see me sometime." I said, "As a matter of fact, Mr. Robinson, I do have an idea that I would like to talk with you about." He said, "Please call my secretary. I would like to hear about it."

Three days later I was sitting in the corner office on the top floor presenting my idea to Mr. Robinson. He did like the idea and wanted to try it. That led to the biggest sales of the year, made me a national sales leader, and sent me to a fancy resort in Puerto Rico. So buy a piece of the rock and sit in the front row.

P.S. You will probably also make money on the stock.

5. *Capitalize on Turnover.* We blow it almost every time. When there is a change in the salesperson on an account, whom does the old salesperson introduce you to? The same low-level guy or gal that they are locked into working with. When this happens, say no, I won't go. The minute you touch the hand of that person, you, too, are locked in at that lower level. Opportunity is knocking. Find someone in your company who can introduce you at a higher level. If there is no one, then use one of the direct approaches to get an appointment with Mr. or Ms. Big. That first contact is all important.

The point is this: When you call at the top, it's easy

to go down to the lower levels of the organization. When you call at the bottom it's difficult—maybe even impossible—to go up and there's another reason for calling at the top. You will find that people are much more receptive if you can say, "Mr./Ms. Big suggested that I work with you on developing _____ _____." It's even more effective if Mr./Ms. Big personally introduces you to the folks downstairs.

6. *Swap Accounts.* Suppose that you have an account where you are locked in at a lower level and you're getting no business and making no progress and that I also have an account with a similar situation. Let's swap. We can both start over by doing the right thing first—call at the top. What have you got to lose? If you're new on the account, you don't know that you're locked in at a lower level.

7. *Take a Picture of the Big Event.* Most words are forgotten by suppertime, but a picture lasts forever. So when you have a big event—when your customer or client is the first, the biggest, the best, or the latest to do something that pertains to your product or service—take a picture of Mr./Ms. Big involved in the action. It could be shown on the six o'clock news, in the local newspaper, or maybe just in the company newsletter.

Any way you mix the ingredients of a big event (a photographer, Mr./Ms. Big, and your product or service) you will be in on the action. And you may be in the picture. At a minimum you'll meet the person at the top. Think of it this way. How many people do you know who don't want their picture in the Sunday paper? And the door will be open for a follow-up call to present a framed enlargement to him or her.

8. *Be a Writer.* This is a kissin' cousin to picture taking. Every industry has its trade magazine. What you want to do is write an article on any big event involving your customer or client that also involves your product or service for publication in the industry's magazine. Here's

the hook. In the article you need some quotes from appropriate people in your customer's company. Those appropriate people include Mr. or Ms. Big. You'll have no trouble seeing the Economic Decision Maker if the purpose of your call is to get his or her name in print. You might even have some suggested quotes prewritten for their approval.

There's also an important fringe benefit. You can use reprints of the article in your marketing to other accounts.

9. *Discover Their Casual Time.* There's no such thing as an 8-to-5 job at the top of the corporate pyramid. They work some crazy hours. But there's often a pattern to their off-hours work. For example, I had an Economic Decision Maker who came to work at 7:00 on Monday morning to organize and plan the week. I had another one who came into the office on Saturday morning in casual dress. What's different and important about these off-hours is that there are no secretaries, no staff people, no barriers between you and them. So just walk in and introduce yourself. That may sound brassy, but it works like a charm. Don't start a sales pitch. Just say, "I have some thoughts about _____ _____ that I would like to review with you sometime." I betcha they say, "Have a seat and tell me about it."

I've observed an important characteristic of these off-hours calls. The customer or prospect appears to be more casual, more attentive, and less hurried. It's as if they are off-duty with their guard down.

And if you're having trouble contacting Mr. or Ms. Big, try calling his or her extension before 8:00 or after 5:00. The switchboard is not open and the secretary is gone. You're likely to get straight through. If you get the security desk, just ask them to put you through to Mr. or Ms. Big. Works like a charm.

10. *Join the Club.* The Country Club, the Rotary Club, the Luncheon Club—that's the feeding ground, the play-

ground, and the home turf of Economic Decision Makers. If you make your home where the buffalo roam, you'll meet a lot of buffalo.

I learned long ago that I rarely had any business problems or competitive problems with those accounts when I was the golfing partner of a decision maker.

TOP SECRET

Chapter 5

½ Day at the CIA

(A Lesson from General George Patton)

Good news! We have openings for a salesperson at two large accounts—the local power company and the local gas company. You can have one of the two accounts. Which one do you want?

When I ask for a show of hands on that question, 80 to 90 percent vote for the power company. Which way would you vote? If you are thinking, "I would really like to know more about the accounts," you are reading the minds of your customers. They also wish you knew more about their business. A focus group of IBM's largest customers said, "Reps (sales representatives) have inadequate knowledge of our business and our industry." A Harvard case study entitled "The Transformation of IBM" quotes a major IBM customer as saying, "They (IBM salespeople) knew nothing about our business, nor did they attempt to learn much." When IBM's largest customers were asked, "What do you expect from a salesperson?" they said that "the number one thing we expect is excellent knowledge of our company, our industry, and the environment in which we do business." When queried about product knowledge, the customers said, "That's in second place." Moreover, their choice of words was interesting. They did not say, "We expect the salesperson to have expert product knowledge, or engineering knowledge, or scientific knowledge." They said instead, "We only expect the rep to *understand* the product line."

So be a specialist in their industry and their business. If you try to be all things to all people, you will be nothing to nobody. This is the age of the expert. The client with the need and the money will gladly pay a premium to increase the probability of success and reduce the risk of failure. That's what you have to offer if you spend one half day at the "CIA." Be the best you can be in the subject that's number one to the customer—his or her business. It's another way to differentiate yourself from your competitor.

As we learned earlier, the more knowledge you have about the customer, the more likely you are to win.

That point was well understood in another field of endeavor by one of the greatest generals in the history of the United States. He said:

I have studied the enemy all my life.
I have read the memoirs of his generals and leaders.
I have read his philosophers.
I have studied in detail every damned one of his battles.
I know exactly how he will react under any circumstance.
So when the time comes I'm going to
whip the hell out of him.

The man who said that was General George S. Patton. A fascinating aside about him is that he could neither read nor write until the age of 12.

So how well do you know your customer? If you can answer the questions in Figure 5.1, you can skip the rest of this chapter. If you're a little short on answers, let's charge straight ahead.

If you were General Patton and you wanted intelligence information, you would go to the CIA. As salespeople wanting knowledge about our customers, we need to spend one half day at the business equivalent of the CIA. That's your local public library. There in public view, at zero cost, you will find the information that will make you number one in the parade of vendors. When you know more about the customer than your competitor does and meet his or her needs better than your competition does, you have, in effect, no competition. In large measure, they sell the best who sell the least but understand the customer the most.

So march right up to the reference desk and ask where you can find the following documents:

1. *U.S. Industrial Outlook.* Here you will find the background, the outlook, the trends, the problems, and the opportunities of 250 industries.
2. *Standard and Poor's Industry Surveys.* This provides additional information and insight by industry.
3. *Value Line Investment Survey.* This source will give you facts, dollars, trends, and business projections for 1700 companies—more information than most employees know about their own company.

HOW WELL DO I KNOW MY CUSTOMER ?

1. My customer's biggest competitor is _____.

2. The single greatest weakness of that competitor is
   _____.

3. The most common complaint or objection to my customer's
   product or service is _____.

4. Pending legislation would affect my customer as follows:
   _____.

5. The single biggest problem in my customer's industry is
   _____.

6. The president's highest priority goal or objective is
   _____.

7. The five-year trend of my customer's market share has been
   _____.

8. My customer's strategy is
   a. Be low cost   b. Product differentiation   c. Niche player

9. The three greatest strengths of my customer's product or
   service are
   a. _____
   b. _____
   c. _____

10. My customer's largest customer is _____.

Figure 5.1   The more you know, the more likely you are to win.

You can shorten your visit to the business CIA by taking these documents to the copy machine. It's not that many pages for one industry or one company.

You will obviously collect the information that pertains to your customer. But don't miss the big trick, which is to collect the same information on your customer's biggest competitor. In calling at the top, we want to act and talk like our competitor is the customer's competitor. You can put yourself in your customer's shoes more effectively if you understand their enemy. If you can see part of the world through his or her eyes, you are more likely to be paid the ultimate compliment by a customer: "You understand our business." That means you have no effective competition. Your competitor is a mere vendor; you, however, are a partner.

If your customer or client is in the public sector, the business CIA also has answers for you. Whether it's the local school system or the police department, their plans, programs, and budgets are a matter of public record. The librarian at the reference desk can direct you to the gold mine of information in the stacks.

There is one additional document we need—the annual report. If it's a public company, the report is easy to get. Just ask. Call up the company's switchboard and say, "Can you direct me to the right person to get a copy of your annual report?" If you really want to do your homework, you can also ask for a copy of the 10-K report. This is a supplement to the annual report filed with the Securities and Exchange Commission. It provides additional and more detailed information on various company activities, extensive financial data (including the earnings and stock holdings of the top officers), and detailed footnotes that do not appear in the annual report.

There are three additional sources of information that will help you think like an insider and not an outsider. A call on the appropriate department will not only get you the information but will also impress them with your interest in their business.

1. Recruiting literature provides an overview of the company, describes its philosophy, paints a picture of its future, and identifies its strengths.
2. Product literature provides insight into the marketing strategy, product line, and product strengths.
3. Company advertising reveals strategy, product positioning, and technical and support strengths.

A final item is the trade or association magazine for your customer's industry. It's usually on the coffee table in the lobby. If you read the editorial page, you will be an instant expert on the burning issue of the day in your client's industry.

If you say, "But I don't have the time to do all of that," let me give you three answers. The first is this: It takes more effort and more sacrifice to live in misery and poverty than is required to achieve success. Secondly, I would remind you of the time you can save by using the Walk-Away Strategy. My third answer will get you more information about your customers than most of them know about themselves: Hire your own corporate cop. That's right. There are private investigators who are in the business of doing for you what the CIA does for generals. Don't get the wrong idea—this is perfectly legal, and all the information is available to the public. These investigators don't fit the image of Sam Spade or Mike Hammer. They are more likely to be an ex-librarian with a computer in the basement that's on-line to a multitude of data bases.

They even have their own club, the Association of Independent Information Professionals, with over 300 members. It's a good bet that there are one or more of these folks in your hometown. You can track them down through their association. Just ask the librarian behind the reference desk to give you their address and phone number from the "Directory of Associations."

Our objective is to increase our effectiveness and account penetration by improving the quality of what we do in high-potential accounts and reduce or eliminate the time we spend in low-potential accounts.

Let me tell you the story of Janet. For the last three years she was the number one salesperson at her company. There was one glaring statistical difference in Janet's sales activity. She averaged only two sales calls per day; the company average was four. Some people said, "Just think how much better she would be if she could just bring her number of calls up to the company average." Wiser people said, "Just think how productive other salespeople could be if they reduced their calls per day."

We started this chapter by saying that over 80 percent of those I poll during seminars vote to have the power company as a customer. So let's spend one half day at the CIA and see what we can learn about the power company. We know that we should also do our homework on the enemy of the power company: the gas company.

What you see summarized in Figure 5.2 is information from the three documents you can find at the library, plus the annual reports of an actual power company and gas company. Let me tell you what we learned.

1. The power company is under intense pressure from environmental groups because of concern over acid rain, the greenhouse effect, radioactive waste disposal, oil spills, and nuclear accidents.

    On the other hand, the gas company will actually benefit from environmental pressure because gas is clean, efficient, and low cost.

2. The power company is one of the top five sinners in the country in their contribution to the acid rain problem. This is because 82 percent of their power is produced from coal, versus 55 percent on a national average for other power companies.

    Not only is the gas company whistle clean, but they have also taken a proactive role and are field-testing gas-powered cars and trucks.

3. The power company is partially dependent on OPEC and the uncertainty of its policies and prices.

    On the other hand, natural gas is all homegrown.

POWER COMPANY	GAS COMPANY
Environmental Pressure Acid rain, greenhouse, radio- active waste, oil spills, nuclear accidents	**Environmental Pressure** Will benefit from environ- mental pressure. Gas is clean, efficient, and low cost.
Clean Air - Acid Rain One of top 5 sinners Coal: 82% vs. 55%	**Clean Air - Acid Rain** Testing gas-powered cars and trucks
Source Dependent on OPEC oil	**Source** Gas is all homegrown
Capacity Critical	**Capacity** Surplus
Projected Growth Low and slow	**Projected Growth** 32,000 New customers/yr. 5,000 Competitive wins/yr.
Earnings Down 16%	**Earnings** 20% Earnings growth
Stock "Unexciting, uncertain"	**Stock** Dividend and earnings should increase annually
Being Sued For: Political contributions Lack of SEC disclosure Improper accounting Negligent conduct	**Lawsuits** NONE

Figure 5.2   Which account would you rather have?

4. The entire power industry faces a capacity problem that could become critical.

   Conversely, there is a *surplus* of gas.

5. The projected growth of the power company can best be described as low and slow.

   The gas company is adding 32,000 new customers per year and is converting an additional 5,000 power customers to gas every year.

6. Earnings for the power company are down 16 percent.

   Earnings for the gas company are increasing at the rate of 20 percent per year.

7. The stock of the power company is judged by professionals to be "unexciting and uncertain" (code words for *sell fast*).

   The dividends and earnings of the gas company are expected to increase annually.

8. The power company has pending lawsuits against it for
   • Unauthorized political contributions
   • Lack of Security and Exchange Commission disclosure
   • Improper accounting practices
   • Negligent conduct
     The gas company has no lawsuits against it.
     Furthermore, the gas company has specific goals to
   • Increase market share
   • Expand service
   • Develop new products
   • Provide good customer service
   • Be highly productive
   • Control cost
   • Control debt

To go back to where we came in—I now ask you, which account would you rather have? After learning the facts, almost all say the gas company. Such is the value of account knowledge and information.

But What About Mr./Ms. Big?

If it's important to know something about the company, it's just as important to know something about the Economic Decision Maker. We'll cover that in depth in the next chapter. But we can get a head start while we're at the CIA. Check out these two documents:

1. *Standard and Poor's Register of Corporations, Directors and Executives*
2. *Marquis Who's Who in the South and Southwest*, etc. (There's a separate book for each geographic part of the country.)

In one or both you're likely to find a listing for the Economic Decision Maker and all sorts of personal and professional information.

For example, if you look under "P" in *Who's Who in the South*, you will find the following:

PEOPLES, DAVID ALEXANDER, writer, speaker; b. Big Rapids, Mich., Aug. 11, 1930; s. Floyd G. and Tressa Z. (Reinhardt) P.; divorced; 1 child, Lisa. BS, U. Tenn., 1955. Mktg. rep. IBM, Chattanooga, 1959–62; sales mgr. IBM, Atlanta, 1962–66; br. mgr. IBM, Greenville, S.C., 1966–72; industry mgr. IBM, Atlanta, 1972–82; consultant, 1982– ; professional. Speaker, 1985– . Author: *Presentations Plus*, 1988 (Maeventec award 1988). 2nd edit., 1992; *Supercharge Your Selling*, 1990. 1st lt. USAF, 1956–59. Mem. ASTD, Nat. Assn. Speakers, Ga. Speakers Assn. Avocations: portrait painting, jogger. *Home and Office: PO Box 8850 Longboat Key FL 34228 (813) 383-0954*

Want to know more? Ask the librarian for the annual issue (which usually comes out in October) of *Business Week* containing the Corporate Elite—a directory of the 1000 largest companies, complete with business and personal information about their CEOs.

And there's still more. Many cities and states have a monthly magazine with a focus on business in that city or that state. Their format includes in-depth stories about local companies, highlighting the executives and the personal side of their lives. It's a good bet that your Mr. or Ms. Big has already been written up in a back issue. You'll find it at the CIA.

You can have what would never occur to your competitor— a personal dossier on your key executive contacts. Knowledge means power, influence, and a winning hand that will differentiate you from your competitor. We'll see how to use these advantages in the next three chapters.

6
Sizing Up Mr./Ms. Big
(Without Ever Having Met Them)

The biggest guns in our sales kit are the executives in our own company. As I said in Chapter 4, they can do for us what we cannot do for ourselves. At IBM, executive calls are more than standard operating procedure. They are part of the corporate culture. But there's good news and bad news associated with having your executives call on your account's executives. The bad news is you have to do your homework. That means preparing a professional account briefing for your executives. The good news is that as a result of the briefing preparation, you will learn more, understand more, and have a better and more comprehensive sales strategy for that account.

But I bet you'll miss the big question. I always did. Your briefing will be characterized by facts, figures, history, and strategy—the kind of information we got from the CIA. All of these are important parts of the briefing, but sooner or later your executive will ask the big question: "What is he/she like? What kind of person is he/she—light and lively, or somber and serious?"

Why is it that our executives have such an intense interest in the body chemistry of the executive they are calling on? The answer lies in the answers to other questions—like those in Figure 6.1.

Or how about this question: Why is it that some people drive a Volvo, others drive a convertible, and still others drive a pickup truck? In fact, some people drive a pickup truck who have no need for one.

Have you ever met someone for the first time, and after just ten minutes you really liked them? On the other hand, think of those people you've met, and after ten minutes you've concluded, "they sure are strange."

Can we predict the behavior of other people?

Do you already know that:

- Bob will give you a decision on the spot?
- Mary will want more study and a written report?
- Jim will want a consensus involving other people?

Why do people act the way they do?

Do people have different buying motives?

Do people have different values for
   * *Style*
   * *Quality*
   * *Technology*
   * *Price*

Figure 6.1 How well do we know our customer's chemistry?

or that:

- Bob will never agree to "X"?
- If Mary said she will be here at 9:00, she will be here at 9:00?
- Jim will always have change for the coffee machine?

Our interest in the body chemistry of the customer executive is motivated by four simple truths:

1. People tend to do business with people they like.
2. The more we are like the customer, the more the customer is likely to do business with us.
3. If we can anticipate the customer's behavior, then we can modify our behavior to be more compatible with them.
4. Don't treat people the way *you* want to be treated. Treat people the way *they* want to be treated. (An important modification to the Golden Rule.)

Is it possible to anticipate the behavior of other people? Is it possible to do this without ever having met them? I will understand if you have a skeptical mind and a raised eyebrow. So let me give you a partial list of the books and the writings that lead us to where we're going:

- *Personal Styles & Effective Performance* by David Merrill and Roger Reid
- *Social Style/Management Style* by Robert and Dorothy Bolton
- *The Versatile Salesperson* by Roger Wenschlag
- The writings and lectures of Dr. Anthony Alessandra

Those of you with an analytical inclination can go back to the writings of the great Swiss psychoanalyst Carl Jung, who coined the words *introvert* and *extrovert*. His book *Psychological Types* laid the foundation for what follows.

The concept we're talking about goes by different names; we will call it *behavioral style.* Its beauty lies in its simplicity. It is not based on deep and mysterious workings of the subconscious but on behavioral characteristics that can be observed by anyone. We tend to judge ourselves by our intentions. But other people cannot feel how we feel or think what we think. They can, however, judge us by what we do and how we behave.

We can size up other people based on their behavior. As we shall see, people tend to have a dominant behavioral style. Once we identify that style, we can then make predictions about their future behavior and reactions. More importantly, we can learn how to modify our behavior to be more compatible and more like them.

We start by determining the general position of an individual on two scales—a vertical and a horizontal. Let's use ourselves as examples as we refer to Figure 6.2.

On the vertical scale we have at the top a person who is *self-contained,* and at the bottom a person who is *open.* As I describe the two, your mission is to decide where you fit on this scale. So pick a number between 1 and 4 that best describes the way you behave. There is, of course, no right or wrong answer. Nor is there any proven advantage to being one way or another. David Merrill and Roger Reid conducted research on the relationship of behavioral style to job performance. They found none. So the message is: Excel at being what you are rather than trying to be what you are not. Behavioral styles are merely a reflection of the reality that different people behave in different ways. It is rare that a person would have 100 percent of the characteristics we will describe, but most people tend to have dominant behavioral characteristics that are observable.

The Self-Contained Person

Self-contained people do not show or share their feelings. They keep their cards close to their chest. They have little hand and

SELF-CONTAINED

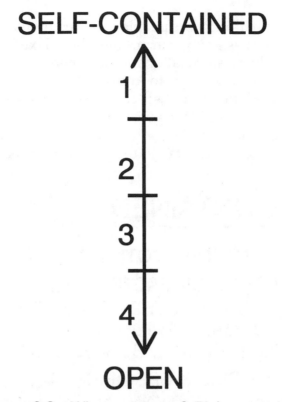

OPEN

Figure 6.2 Where are you? Pick a number.

body movement and limited facial expression, tending to keep their distance both physically and mentally; they don't touch, and they don't like to be touched. Their focus tends to be on facts and logic. They appear more task-oriented than people-oriented. Formal, serious, and rigid, they come across as impersonal and "all business." Their discussions tend to be precise and specific. They are generally viewed as being hard to get to know because they avoid personal involvement.

The Open Person

You can read open people like a book. They show and share their emotions in what they say, in their body language, and in their facial expression. They use their intuition and listen to that little voice within. More people-oriented then task-oriented, they come across as being warm, friendly, relaxed, personable, and informal. They are relationship-oriented and are generally viewed as being easy to get to know.

The characteristics of the self-contained person and the open person are summarized in Figure 6.3.

On the horizontal scale we have on the far right a person who is *direct* and on the far left a person who is *indirect*. As

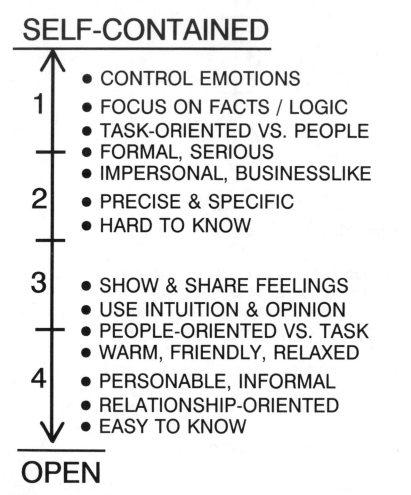

SELF-CONTAINED

1
- CONTROL EMOTIONS
- FOCUS ON FACTS / LOGIC
- TASK-ORIENTED VS. PEOPLE
- FORMAL, SERIOUS
- IMPERSONAL, BUSINESSLIKE

2
- PRECISE & SPECIFIC
- HARD TO KNOW

3
- SHOW & SHARE FEELINGS
- USE INTUITION & OPINION
- PEOPLE-ORIENTED VS. TASK
- WARM, FRIENDLY, RELAXED

4
- PERSONABLE, INFORMAL
- RELATIONSHIP-ORIENTED
- EASY TO KNOW

OPEN

Figure 6.3   Pick a number.

we describe these two extremes, your next mission is to pick a letter from Figure 6.4. Are you more like an A, B, C, or D?

The Direct Person

Direct people are highly assertive and tend to come on strong. They are decisive in their behavior and usually make quick decisions. They clearly operate more in a "tell" mode than an "ask and listen" mode. There is a tendency to speak quickly, intensely, and often loudly. They are confident in what they say and therefore say it emphatically. They like to do most of the talking.

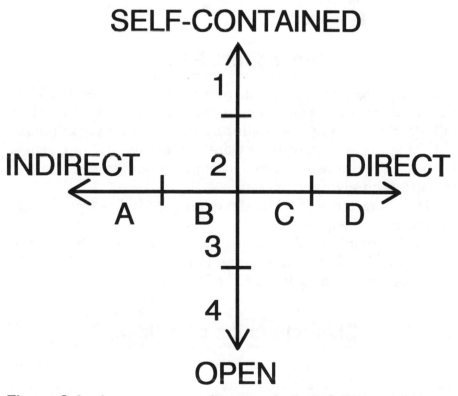

Figure 6.4 Are you more direct or indirect? Pick a letter.

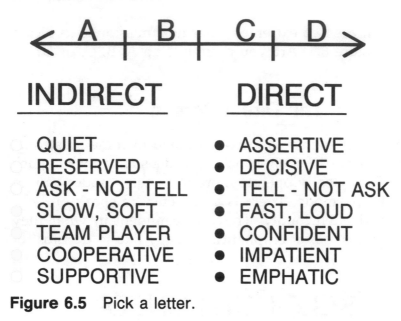

Figure 6.5   Pick a letter.

The Indirect Person

Indirect people come across as more quiet and reserved. They tend to ask questions and listen more than they talk. They often talk slowly and softly, meditating on their decisions to minimize risk. They are team players who are cooperative and supportive. Overall they are less forceful in expressing opinions, making requests, and giving directions.

The characteristics of the direct and the indirect person are summarized in Figure 6.5.

At this point we should have a number from the vertical scale and a letter from the horizontal scale.

If you are a 1 or 2 and a C or D, then you are a *Driver*.

Characteristics of a Driver

Drivers are determined, demanding, and decisive. They are independent and self-directed. They know what they want, and they want it yesterday. Their focus is on facts and logic. They are risk takers, and they make decisions more quickly than all

DRIVER

☑ DETERMINED, DEMANDING, DECISIVE

☑ INDEPENDENT, SELF-DIRECTED

☑ KNOWS WHAT THEY WANT

☑ WANTS IT <u>YESTERDAY</u>

☑ FOCUS IS ON FACTS, LOGIC

☑ RISK TAKER

☑ MAKES FAST DECISIONS

☑ ACTION- AND RESULTS-ORIENTED

☑ NOT PEOPLE-ORIENTED

☑ TELL-ORIENTED, NOT ASK-ORIENTED

☑ STUBBORN AND IMPATIENT

☑ SEEKS POWER AND CONTROL

Figure 6.6 The characteristics of a Driver.

the other behavior types. They will often make a decision after only one or two contacts. They are action- and results-oriented, not people-oriented. Their modus operandi is to tell, not ask. They can be stubborn and impatient. They seek power, control, and authority. If they had a theme song it would be "My Way," and their motto would be "Show me bottom-line results." The only time they would say "well done" is when they order a steak. They tend to like pressure and deadlines, so they are often found in occupations that have these characteristics. They make good CEOs, monarchs, and dictators. It is thought that they make up 15 percent of the population. A Driver is usually sold on the first or second call.

The characteristics of a Driver are summarized in Figure 6.6.

If you are a 1 or 2 and an A or B, then you are an Analytical.

Characteristics of an Analytical

Analyticals are objective, deliberate, and cautious. They are serious, exacting, and persistent. They like order, structure, and procedure. They tend to focus on an analysis of the facts, and they are well known for attention to details and complete staff work. As a result, they minimize risk. They are skeptical and want proof. They are good at planning, organizing, and problem solving. Because they want a lot of information, they are "ask" oriented—not "tell"-oriented. They are, however, somewhat impersonal and detached. They are the slowest decision makers, requiring five to seven contacts to sell. Analyticals gravitate to the professions that are exact sciences, i.e., engineering, architecture, accounting, and so on. They make up approximately 35 percent of the population.

The characteristics of an Analytical are summarized in Figure 6.7.

If you are a 3 or 4 and an A or B, then you are an Amiable.

Characteristics of an Amiable

Amiables are warm, friendly, and dependable. They are loyal, dedicated, and cooperative. Amiables are people-, team-, and

ANALYTICAL

☑ OBJECTIVE, DELIBERATE, CAUTIOUS

☑ SERIOUS, EXACTING, PERSISTENT

☑ LIKES ORDER AND STRUCTURE

☑ FOCUS IS ON ANALYSIS OF FACTS

☑ COMPLETED STAFF WORK

☑ ATTENTION TO DETAIL

☑ SKEPTICAL, WANTS PROOF

☑ GOOD PROBLEM SOLVER

☑ GOOD PLANNER AND ORGANIZER

☑ ASK-ORIENTED, NOT TELL-ORIENTED

☑ AVOIDS RISK

☑ IMPERSONAL, DETACHED

Figure 6.7   The characteristics of an Analytical.

relationship-oriented. They are good listeners with great sensitivity to the feelings of others. They are the very best at customer service. Amiables will tend to avoid conflict and controversy. They like to get other people involved in decision making and obtain a group consensus. They are interested in low risk and guarantees. It will probably take four to five contacts to sell an Amiable. Amiables are common in occupations that have a people orientation like sales, psychiatry, the ministry, medicine, nursing, and so on. They make up approximately 35 percent of the population. Some say they are the best lovers.

The characteristics of an Amiable are summarized in Figure 6.8.

If you are a 3 or 4 and a C or D, then you are an Expressive.

Characteristics of an Expressive

Expressives are enthusiastic, dramatic, and inspiring. They are fun-loving and flamboyant people. Many of their actions are spontaneous, with a tendency to be impulsive. They place great reliance on their intuition and hunches. They are very persuasive, so they are well suited for sales careers. They can get other people excited about their ideas. Expressives have a history of talking themselves into and out of almost anything. They are innovative and creative. They are the dreamers. They are interested in the big picture, not the details. Their desire for visibility and recognition leads them to want to be the biggest, the best, or the first. They are risk takers. They will make a decision after only two or three contacts. They spend a lot of time talking about their favorite subject—themselves—and are believed to represent about 15 percent of the population. They are often found in politics, in sales, and in the entertainment industry.

I said that Amiables are the best lovers. That's not exactly correct. They are tied with Expressives for that title. Amiables are the best lovers in terms of quality, whereas Expressives are the best lovers in terms of quantity. So they say.

AMIABLE

☑ WARM, FRIENDLY, DEPENDABLE

☑ LOYAL, DEDICATED, COOPERATIVE

☑ PEOPLE- AND TEAM-ORIENTED

☑ RELATIONSHIP-ORIENTED

☑ SENSITIVE TO FEELINGS

☑ GOOD LISTENER

☑ BEST AT CUSTOMER SERVICE

☑ AVOIDS CONFLICT AND CONTROVERSY

☑ WANTS GROUP CONSENSUS

☑ LIKES GUARANTEES, LOW RISK

Figure 6.8   The characteristics of an Amiable.

EXPRESSIVE

☑ ENTHUSIASTIC, DRAMATIC, INSPIRING

☑ FLAMBOYANT AND FUN-LOVING

☑ IMPULSIVE AND SPONTANEOUS

☑ RELIES ON INTUITION AND HUNCHES

☑ VERY PERSUASIVE

☑ INNOVATIVE AND CREATIVE

☑ AN IDEA PERSON, A DREAMER

☑ ORIENTED TO BIG PICTURE, NOT DETAILS

☑ SEEKS RECOGNITION AND VISIBILITY

☑ WANTS TO BE FIRST

☑ IMPERSONAL, DETACHED

Figure 6.9 The characteristics of an Expressive.

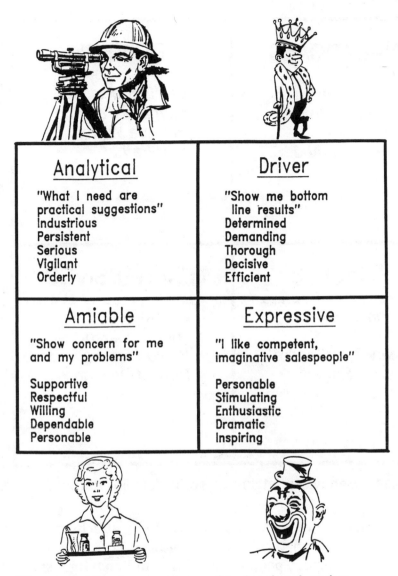

Figure 6.10   A summary of behavioral styles.

The characteristics of an Expressive are summarized in Figure 6.9.

If we were to summarize some of the more salient characteristics of the four behavior styles, it would look like Figure 6.10.

ANALYTICALS	DRIVERS
Albert Einstein *Sherlock Holmes* *Mr. Spock* *Queen Elizabeth*	*Lee Iacocca* *Margaret Thatcher* *Barbara Walters* *Dan Rather*
AMIABLES	EXPRESSIVES
John Denver *Gerald Ford* *Mary Tyler Moore* *Kenny Rogers*	*Liza Minelli* *Johnny Carson* *Pablo Picasso* *Ronald Reagan*

Figure 6.11   Behavioral styles of some familiar names.

We can bring the behavioral styles to life by attaching some familiar names to them, as shown in Figure 6.11.

As you might expect, people with different behavioral styles would tend to drive different automobiles, like those in Figure 6.12.

If we were to assign behavioral styles to the animal kingdom, we would find something like Figure 6.13.

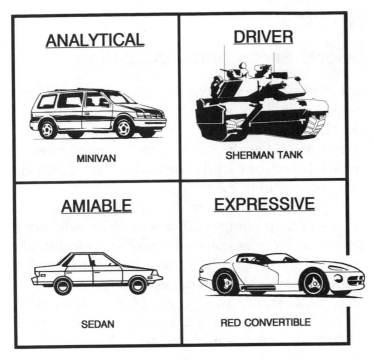

Figure 6.12 Favored transportation of behavioral styles.

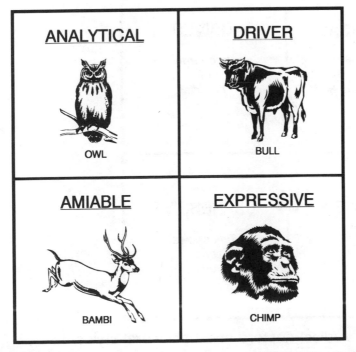

Figure 6.13 Behavioral styles of the animal kingdom.

Behavioral Styles and Occupations

As I described each behavioral style, I gave examples of occupations for which each is suited. You need to note, however, that all behavioral styles are to be found in most occupations. For a lot of us, our career selection was affected by many internal and external factors. In fact, one study concluded that 62 percent of us fall into our occupations by accident.

Nevertheless, people do tend to be attracted to certain professions because of their compatibility with their behavioral style. Fortunately, many professions offer sound opportunities for all four behavioral styles. Consider, for example, the perfect blend of career and behavioral style that is available to medical doctors or to lawyers, as shown in Figure 6.14 and Figure 6.15.

This is all very interesting, but what does it mean to you? Why is it important, and how would you use it?

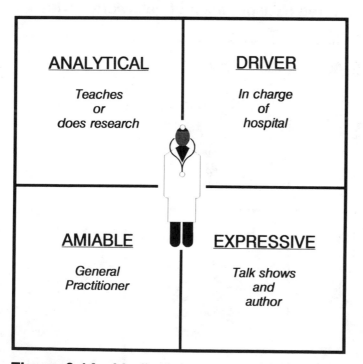

Figure 6.14   Medical doctors and behavioral styles.

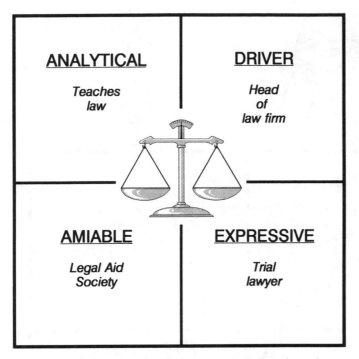

Figure 6.15   Lawyers and behavioral styles.

It's important because of a seven-year study of the success factors of outstanding salespeople by David Mayer and Herbert Greenberg. They found two—only two—success factors:

1. Ego drive
2. A large amount of empathy

Listen to what their study said about empathy: "The important ability to feel as the other fellow does in order to be able to sell him [sic] a product or service must be possessed in large measure."

Here's the problem. If you are a Driver or Expressive, 85 percent of your customers or clients are very different from you. If you are an Analytical or Amiable, 65 percent are different from you. Consider also that a particular behavioral style can be seen and described in either positive or negative terms. Let's

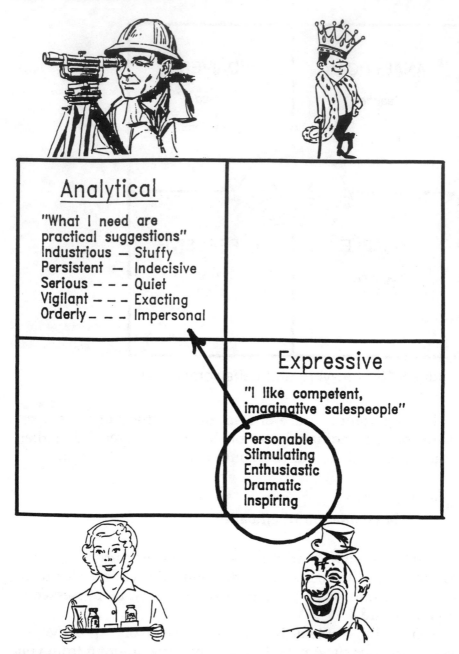

Figure 6.16   If the executive is an Expressive and you are an Analytical.

look at Figure 6.16. If the executive you are calling on is an Expressive and you are an Analytical, how would they see you? Do you think you would be perceived as industrious, persistent, serious, vigilant, and orderly? Probably not. They would instead see the negative side and view you as stuffy, indecisive, quiet, exacting, and impersonal.

On the other hand, if the executive is an Analytical and you are the Expressive, then you are likely to be seen as opinionated, excitable, reactive, undisciplined, and promotional (Figure 6.17).

If the executive is a Driver and you are an Amiable, you are probably seen as conforming, retiring, indecisive, emotional, and weak, as shown in Figure 6.18.

But if the executive is an Amiable and you are a Driver, then you are pushy, severe, dominating, mean, and harsh, as shown in Figure 6.19.

Behavior Modification

Clearly there is a need to modify our behavior if we are to be effective with other behavior styles.

I had earlier made reference to a study that found no connection between people's behavioral styles and their job success. But that same study found that what consistently separated high performers and low performers was that the high performers were rated as having high interpersonal versatility. That's a fancy way of saying that they were skilled in modifying their behavior in order to be more compatible with the behavioral characteristics of the other party.

Another study compared 21 derailed executives to a group who made it all the way to the top. One difference stood out: Those who had succeeded had the ability to understand other people's perspectives.

The primary factor in occupational success is the ability to work well with people. Research aimed at discovering the primary reason for the termination of employees has provided surprisingly consistent results. Approximately 80 percent are released because of poor interpersonal relationships on the job.

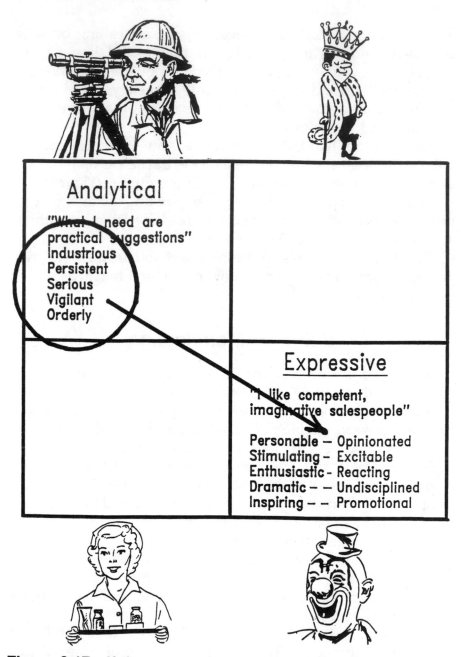

Analytical

"What I need are
practical suggestions"
Industrious
Persistent
Serious
Vigilant
Orderly

Expressive

"I like competent,
imaginative salespeople"

Personable – Opinionated
Stimulating – Excitable
Enthusiastic - Reacting
Dramatic – – Undisciplined
Inspiring – – Promotional

Figure 6.17   If the executive is an Analytical and you are
an Expressive.

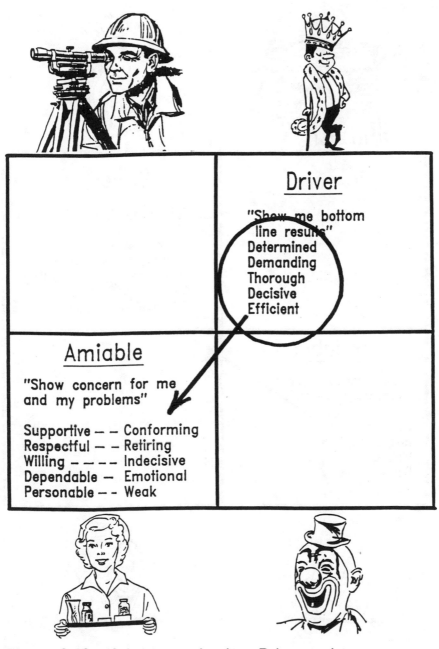

Figure 6.18   If the executive is a Driver and you are an Amiable.

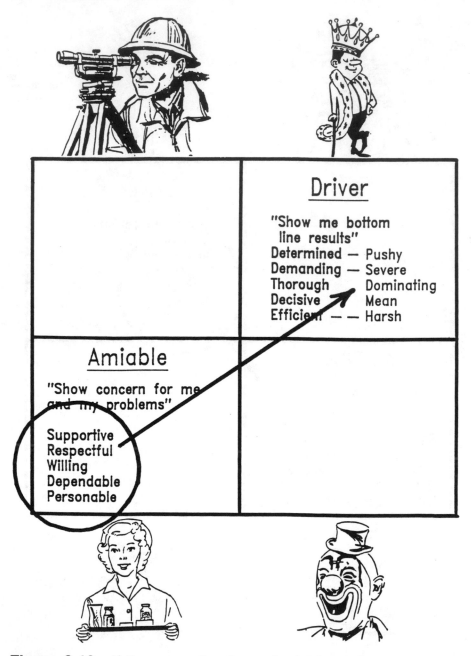

Figure 6.19 If the executive is an Amiable and you are a Driver.

We should not be surprised because, as mentioned earlier, 65 to 85 percent of the people who are important to our success are very different from us.

All of us modify our behavior to some degree without even thinking about it. We are more likely to engage in small talk with Jane who enjoys it, but we get right down to business with John because we know he prefers it that way. I am talking about using good judgment and behavior modification, not a major personality change. This is the same good judgment one would use in refraining from smoking in the office of a nonsmoker.

We can all be successful when calling on people just like us. But most of the world is not like us. We need to communicate in their language, not ours. We are more likely to be successful if we treat people the way they want to be treated—not the way *we* want to be treated.

The implications for salespeople are dramatic. You would think, for example, that Expressives would make the best salespeople. In fact, any group of salespeople will contain more Expressives than any other behavior style. Nevertheless, all behavioral styles are represented in groups of salespeople. It is interesting, however, that the star performers are not predominantly Expressives. People with other behavioral styles attain superstar performance because of their skill in modifying their behavior to be compatible with their clients or their customers. And you can too. The kind of behavior modification I am talking about is summarized in Figure 6.20.

The next four pages provide details and specific suggestions for calling on each behavior style (Figures 6.21, 6.22, 6.23, and 6.24).

For each style I make suggestions about

- How to open the call
- How to conduct the call
- What to do
- What *not* to do
- Their probable business buying reasons
- Their probable personal buying reasons

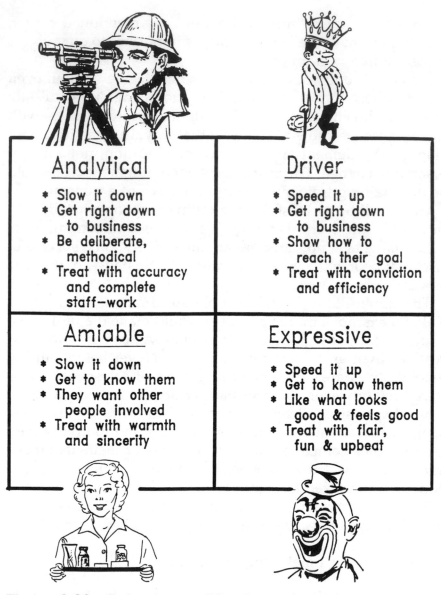

Analytical
* Slow it down
* Get right down
    to business
* Be deliberate,
    methodical
* Treat with accuracy
    and complete
    staff—work

Driver
* Speed it up
* Get right down
    to business
* Show how to
    reach their goal
* Treat with conviction
    and efficiency

Amiable
* Slow it down
* Get to know them
* They want other
    people involved
* Treat with warmth
    and sincerity

Expressive
* Speed it up
* Get to know them
* Like what looks
    good & feels good
* Treat with flair,
    fun & upbeat

Figure 6.20 Behavior modification to improve effectiveness.

Open the Call

- Listen to their objectives
- Address specific problems
- Be personable, but reserved
- Present facts and evidence

Conduct the Call

- Speed it up
- Get right down to business
- Focus on their goals
- Treat with conviction

Do

- Be clear, specific and brief
- Stick to business
- Be prepared and organized
- Provide alternatives
- Give facts to compare
- Have facts about risk
- Focus on results
- Ask, don't tell
- Clarify priorities
- Anticipate objections

Don't

- Ramble
- Waste their time
- Play it by ear
- Leave loopholes
- Have all the answers
- Speculate
- Overwhelm with detail
- Beat around the bush
- Have surprises
- Be personal

Business Buying Reasons

- Bottom line results
- Gets the job done
- On schedule, under budget

Personal Buying Reasons

- More personal power
- Increase control
- Choice of options

Figure 6.21   How to call on a Driver.

ANALYTICAL

Open the Call

- Establish your credibility
- Give your credentials
- Acknowledge their expert status
- Give "case study" examples

Conduct the Call

- Slow it down
- Be deliberate, methodical
- Be factual and accurate
- Completed staff work

Do

- Be well prepared
- Stick to business
- Discuss pros and cons
- Minimize risk
- Have detailed plan
- Provide solid evidence
- Be realistic with schedules
- Stress cost effectiveness
- Be thorough and unhurried
- Be decisive and specific

Don't

- Be unprepared or disorganized
- Be casual, informal, or loud
- Rush
- Play it by ear
- Use unreliable references
- Use opinion as evidence
- Be clever, or use gimmicks
- Guess if you don't know
- Use personal appeals
- Use users as evidence

Business Buying Reasons

- Meets specifications
- Meets goals/objectives
- Most logical solution

Personal Buying Reasons

- Respected as expert
- Pride in staffwork
- Need to be "right"

Figure 6.22   How to call on an Analytical.

Open the Call

- Engage in informal talk before getting down to business
- Show interest in their work/goals
- Reference people they may know

Conduct the Call

- Slow it down
- Get to know them
- They will want others involved
- Treat with warmth, sincerity

Do

- Start with ice-breaker
- Show interest in them
- Find common areas
- Listen, be responsive
- Ask "How?" questions
- Move casually, informally
- Focus on low risk
- Provide personal assurances
- Give verbal/nonverbal feedback
- Ask who else will be involved

Don't

- Rush headlong into business
- Stick coldly to business
- Say "Here's how I see it"
- Be domineering/demanding
- Debate facts and figures
- Be abrupt and rapid
- Be vague
- Offer options/probabilities
- Offer opinions
- Be formal, reserved

Business Buying Reasons

- Staff/Committee approval
- Guarantees/Assurances
- Tried and proven

Personal Buying Reasons

- Like, trust, respect
- Group consensus
- Avoids conflict/controversy

Figure 6.23 How to call on an Amiable.

Open the Call

- Describe purpose of call
- Establish credibility
- Discuss people they know
- Share exclusive information

Conduct the Call

- Speed it up
- Get to know them
- Make it look/sound good
- Treat with flair, fun, upbeat

Do

- Support their dreams
- Plan to socialize, relate
- Talk about people
- Ask for their opinions
- Provide implementation plan
- Be stimulating, fun loving
- Keep it fast moving
- Use prominent references
- Offer special incentives for their willingness to take a risk

Don't

- Overwhelm with detail
- Legislate
- Be curt and cold
- Be tight lipped
- Dwell on facts and figures
- Be impersonal, judgmental
- Be task-oriented
- Be dogmatic
- Fail to give plenty of verbal and nonverbal feedback

Business Buying Reasons

- Creative idea, big deal
- Good references
- Sounds and feels good

Personal Buying Reasons

- Recognition/Publicity
- Be first, biggest, best
- Innovative/Unique

Figure 6.24 How to call on an Expressive.

The Big Problem—Two Solutions

Now you've got the answers, but you don't know the question: What is the behavioral style of our Mr. or Ms. Big? If you've never met him or her, you wouldn't have the faintest idea. What to do?

There are two different techniques you can use to determine the behavioral style of individuals without ever having met them.

One approach is to interview someone who does know them (like the Coach) and ask them four questions that are shown along with their possible answers in Figure 6.25. When you circle the answers you are given, a clear pattern will usually emerge that will tell you their probable behavioral style.

A second way to determine behavioral style is to talk to the individual on the phone. This could be when you are asking for an appointment, as discussed in Chapter 4. Listen to how he or she answers the question "Am I calling at a good time?" Then, as the conversation continues, listen carefully to the characteristics of how he or she talks, as shown in Figure 6.26. Again, a pattern should emerge that will tell you the probable behavioral style.

There we have it—the answer to the big questions "What are they like? What kind of person are they?" You can now predict and anticipate the behavior of the executive you will be calling on. Consequently, you have the answers to two important questions: How should you conduct yourself on the call, and how should you modify your behavior? It will be helpful if you clearly understand your sales strengths and weaknesses as shown in Figure 6.27. The answers to the above questions are another important step in improving your effectiveness and in differentiating yourself from your competitors.

"SIZE" UP WITH FOUR QUESTIONS

DRIVER	ANALYTICAL	AMIABLE	EXPRESSIVE

#1 "What is their background?"

DRIVER	ANALYTICAL	AMIABLE	EXPRESSIVE
Entrepreneurial Technical	Science Technical	Public Contact Liberal Arts	Sales Liberal Arts

#2 "How do they dress?"

DRIVER	ANALYTICAL	AMIABLE	EXPRESSIVE
Conservative	Conservative	Casual	Flamboyant

#3 "How does their office look?"

DRIVER	ANALYTICAL	AMIABLE	EXPRESSIVE
Large desk Clean Clock Awards No posters	Diplomas Symbols of achievement Plaques Stacks of paper	Home-like Family pictures Plants Posters Mementos	Messy desk Trophies Posters Pictures with celebrities

#4 "What adjectives would you use to describe him/her?"

DRIVER	ANALYTICAL	AMIABLE	EXPRESSIVE
Decisive Demanding Pushy Efficient Dominating Determined Strong-willed Action-oriented	Persistent Serious Industrious Orderly Procedures Exacting Quiet Impersonal	Personable Friendly Agreeable Respectful Supportive Trusts and Believes in others	Excitable Dramatic Enthusiastic Inspiring Persuasive Stimulating Impulsive Promotional

Figure 6.25 Determining behavior style by asking four questions.

"SIZE" UP WITH A PHONE CALL

"Am I calling at a good time?"

DRIVER	ANALYTICAL	AMIABLE	EXPRESSIVE
"How long will this take?"	They preplan an out.	"As good as possible."	"Yes, it is."
"Well, what do you need?"	"I've got a meeting in a few minutes."	"As good as any."	"Sure." "Fine."
	"How long will it take?" 	"Yes, this is O.K." 	
Fuller volume	Lower volume	Lower volume	Fuller volume
Rapid speech	Slower speech	Slower speech	Rapid speech
Rapid response	Unhurried response	Unhurried response	Rapid response
Little inflection	No inflection	Moderate inflection	Lots of inflection
Low pitch	Low pitch	Moderate pitch	Moderate/ High pitch
Authoritative tone	Serious/ formal tone	Calm tone	Friendly/ Lively tone
Few pauses	Long pauses	No pauses	Many pauses
Moderate # of words	Brief Concise	Moderate # of words	Rambling words

Figure 6.26 Determining behavioral style by how they talk.

	STRENGTHS	*WEAKNESSES*
DRIVER	Aggressive Persistent Hard worker Desire to win Asks for the order	Dominates Impatient Talks too fast Intimidates Promises too much
ANALYTICAL	Well prepared Competent Good follow-up Good service Diplomatic	Too cautious Not competitive Too much detail Confuses client Hurt by rejection
AMIABLE	Warm & friendly Good listener Likeable Well prepared Good service	Lacks killer instinct Inflexible Resists change Possessive Objection handling
EXPRESSIVE	Persuasive Self-confident Enthusiastic Natural in sales Motivational	Too optimistic Talks too much Promises too much Poor listener Hurt by rejection

Figure 6.27 Selling strengths and weaknesses of behavioral styles.

7
What to Talk About?
(Answer: What's Important to Them)

To better understand top executives and gain some insight into what's important to them, let's look at the different ways that they get the information they need to run their railroads. A study by John Rockart at MIT lists five techniques executives use to obtain management information.

The By-product Technique

This method is the most common. The management information is produced as a by-product of performing a basic business function. For example, an analysis of actual versus budgeted expenditures can be developed during the course of performing the basic accounting functions. Other examples might be identifying actual versus forecasted sales or the top ten and bottom ten customers as a result of doing sales analysis. Or you could list delinquencies by time duration as a by-product of doing the bookkeeping for accounts receivable.

The good news about this technique is that it's cheap and efficient. The bad news is that the information may not be focused on the needs of the business, and there is often too much information of limited value.

The Confidant Approach

This technique is personal and informal. It relies on word of mouth from an inner circle of trusted advisors, like the president's cabinet. It is predicated on the assumption that business is dynamic and ever changing and that its information needs cannot be predetermined. It tends to be subjective—often based on impressions, feelings, and that little voice within. It is only as good as the knowledge and judgment of the giver.

The Key Indicator System

All the items that are judged to be important in the business are measured and tracked. This was a common technique at

IBM. As a branch manager, I was measured on 29 different items—everything from revenue and new accounts to accounts receivable delinquencies. There are two problems with this system. The first is that when you are trying to watch 29 trees, you can't see the forest. The second problem is that when you emphasize everything, you emphasize nothing.

The "Big Study"

Here is the consultant's gold mine: a study conducted over three, six, or nine months that is to provide all the answers to all the problems. It consists of interviews at all levels to determine future wants and needs versus today's reality. Then a total system is designed to give everybody what they say they need (or want).

The resultant new system is usually expensive and often requires a new bureaucracy. Moreover, implementation may take a couple of years. Therein lies its greatest weakness. By the time the study is completed and the new system is fully operational, many of the problems it was meant to solve may no longer exist. For example, what if

- Supplier quality has already improved
- A weaker dollar has increased exports
- New legislation solved an environmental problem
- Business recovery now means more hiring, not downsizing
- Product redesign has already solved the parts problem
- Your biggest competitor has gone bankrupt

Critical Success Factors

The concept of Critical Success Factors (CSFs) was originally conceived by Arthur Andersen and was later refined by McKinsey & Company. Then John Rockart at MIT's Sloan School of Management took it a step further. He used CSFs to define the information needs of key decision makers. These factors then became the basis for a company's management information system and provided the standards for performance measurements. The concept has been so successful that its use is now widespread. Its beauty lies in its simplicity.

Critical Success Factors are those few things that must go absolutely right for an organization to succeed and prosper.

In most companies you can count the CSFs on your fingers and have fingers left over. Usually only three to six items will determine success. If these are performed well, the company will prosper; if not, the company will fail. Everything else can be mediocre.

Let's consider the automobile industry. The United States lost a large part of its automobile industry to the Japanese. Why? If you were to ask people to give you a one-word answer to the question "What is the biggest difference between a Japanese car and a Detroit car?" most people would reply, "Quality." Quality is one of the Critical Success Factors in the automobile industry. The others are

- Styling
- Strong dealer network
- Cost control

If these four things are done well, Detroit will prosper. To the extent they are done poorly, it would lose market share.

In the supermarket business the Critical Success Factors are

- Price
- Product mix
- Sales promotion
- Inventory control

Some people say there is a fifth factor—Cleanliness. Other examples of CSFs for different industries are

Steel . . . . Cost control
Cereal . . . . Advertising
Soft drinks . . . . Distribution network
Computers . . . . New products

Critical Success Factors can and do vary over time. For example, in the days of fuel shortages and high prices, fuel efficiency was a CSF in the automobile industry.

CSFs can also vary within the same industry. For example, what is critical to Wal-Mart is very different from what is critical to Neiman Marcus.

Is this a big deal? Let me give you two answers. The first answer comes from a philosopher:

As you wander through this life, my friend,
Whatever be your goal,
Keep your eye upon the donut (CSF)
And not upon the hole.

The second answer could come from an MBA, who would say that CSFs perform these functions:

- Provide managerial focus
- Serve as a catalyst for management activity
- Define the threats and opportunities for the business
- Allow a company to evaluate its strengths and weaknesses
- Allow an alignment of resources with objectives
- Define the information needs of the business

Now back to where we came in: What to talk about? The answer is, talk about what's important to him or her: their Critical Success Factors. Your mission is to find a way to relate your product or service to their CSFs. If you do that, your product or service will have more value, *you* will have more value, and you will have an open door to the corner office.

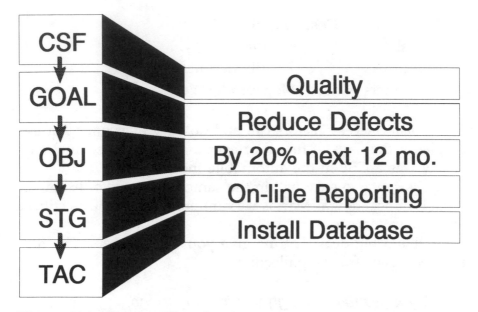

Figure 7.1 Don't sell a database to an executive at the top. Sell better quality (CSF).

How do I determine the CSFs for my customers? If you have spent a half day at the CIA, you will have enough information to make a very educated guess as to the CSFs for your customer. Then on the first call, if you ask the right questions, you will hear the CSFs from the horse's mouth. Your work at the CIA will help you to ask the right questions.

And now for the next subject: What are your customer's goals and objectives? Wait a minute. I'm confused. What's the difference between goals, objectives, and Critical Success Factors?

Let's take a look at Figure 7.1 and see if you can sort out the protocol.

First you would look at the company's Critical Success Factors; let's say quality is one of them. Next you would consider the company's goals, which would be a subset of the CSF. If quality is a CSF, then one of your goals might be to help the company reduce defects. Next are the company's objectives. By definition, objectives are measurable within a given time period.

So in this example, your objective might be to reduce defects by 20 percent within the next 12 months. One strategy to accomplish this might be an on-line defect reporting system, and your tactic to implement this might be to install a database system.

In summary, you might think of it this way:

1. CSF—What destination is important?
2. GOAL—The direction to go to get there
3. OBJECTIVE—The speed of travel and time of arrival
4. STRATEGY—The vehicle to drive
5. TACTIC—The fuel to use

Here's the point. If your product or service is a database system, don't try to sell that to an executive at the top. Instead, sell better quality—for which they have a company goal with specific objectives. If you try to sell the database system at the top, you are likely to get sent downstairs. The language at the top consists of CSFs, goals, and objectives—not implementation tactics.

Now, back to your customer's goals and objectives. Here's the best news of the day. You'll find your customer's goals and objectives written in plain English in a public document for publicly held companies. They're on page 2 of the Annual Report. (Page 1 is full of numbers.) Page 2 is the letter to the stockholders from the CEO. It will always tell you what's important to the top management.

Remember the gas company and the power company? The letter to stockholders in the annual report of the gas company says, "Our goals are to increase our market share, expand into new areas, support economic development, and maintain high standards of customer service."

The CEO of the power company says, "I want us to change the way we've always done business. . . . I want our customers to think of us as providing extraordinary service." How's that for an open door?

The strategy you should consider for your first call at the top is one that sells yourself, not your product or service. The best way to do this is to demonstrate a knowledge of their business and a sincere desire to be of service in areas that are important to the customer. This is most effectively done by asking well-thought out questions that reflect a knowledge of their business and an interest in their goals—questions that by their content reflect a desire and an ability to be of more service and of greater value than a mere "vendor." Questions, interest, and knowledge are the building blocks of a business partnership.

To confirm your customer's CSFs, you have to ask the right questions of the right person. If you ask the wrong person, you may find out what's critical for a department or a division but not for the company. If, for example, you ask "B" in Figure 7.2, you may be told that production, maintenance, and backlog are critical. And they are—for "B's" department. Only "A" can tell us that quality, cost control, and styling are critical for the company. One person's floor is another person's ceiling.

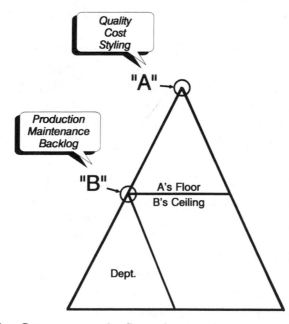

Figure 7.2   One person's floor is another person's ceiling.

Asking the right questions is not always as easy as you might think. Your customer may not be familiar with CSF terminology. Figure 7.3 has some questions to ask that will get you the information you need and uncover significant problems. You should then discuss the importance of the problems, quantify their seriousness, and determine their impact on the business. You are laying the groundwork for offering solutions to real problems that the customer has agreed are significant and critical. This discussion is the foundation for getting a "yes" answer to the "Will Buy" question. We don't want to present a solution to a problem that the customer doesn't feel he or she has.

You can sound like a consultant if you use their language when you ask questions:

- What do you like best/least about . . . ?
- How do you feel about . . . ?
- In your opinion, what is . . . ?
- What do you think about . . . ?
- What would it mean to you if . . . ?
- Can you be more specific about . . . ?
- Could you elaborate on . . . ?
- How are you doing it now?
- What are the results?
- What results would you like?
- Do I understand correctly that you . . . ?

- *What are the priority issues in your business?*

- *What goals have you identified with respect to these issues?*

- *How would you prioritize these goals?*

- *What specifically has to go right to achieve your goals?*

- *What are the barriers to achieving your goals?*

- *How do you monitor your perfor-mance in achieving your goals?*

Figure 7.3 How to ask ''What's important?''

- What might have accounted for . . . ?
- What prompted your decision to . . . ?
- How did you happen to . . . ?

And don't forget the phrases most commonly used by consultants:

- Tell me a little more about . . .
- Others in similar situations have found that . . .
- I can understand why you would feel that way about . . .

The Hardest Thing in the World to Do

As you read this, there are thousands of sales calls taking place all over the country. If you could open the door and look in on one of those sales calls, who would be doing the talking? Eighty percent of the time it's the salesperson. Stated another way, the salesperson talks four out of five minutes of the average sales call. Yet there is an inverse relationship between your talk time and your effectiveness. You will be much more effective if you talk 20 percent of the time. And most of that 20 percent should be spent asking questions.

What should you do the other 80 percent of the time? You do what is almost (not quite, but almost) impossible—you listen. The biggest difference between consultants and salespeople is that consultants question and listen, whereas salespeople talk.

And we are not alone. Carl Bernstein, who along with Bob Woodward broke the Watergate story by questioning and listening, says, "The problem with reporters today is they don't listen."

IBM's customers are equally vocal in their criticism: "They (IBM) never asked about our needs. They don't listen." "Instead of asking us what we need or want, they tell us what we should do with what IBM has already dictated. . . ."

As a member of the National Speakers Association, I frequently attend its conventions. At one convention I went to a break-out session on listening. I thought it would be empty. It was packed. Professional speakers understand the need for and the value of listening.

When you talk, you only learn what you already know. When you question and listen, you learn your customer's problems, needs, priorities, values, and buying criteria. You learn what he or she wants. The secret to selling is not creating interest but discovering the interest that already exists. And the easiest (and fastest) way to sell is to solve their problem or give them what they want. Your questions will be determined by your product or service. But here are some examples of the kinds of things to ask about and listen for:

In the area of management
- Goals, objectives
- Planning, strategy
- Internal focus, customer focus

In the area of manufacturing/distribution
- Inventory
- Stock turn
- Quality control
- Scrap rate
- Late shipments

In the area of financial performance
- Margins
- Price/earnings ratio
- Cash flow
- Bad debt write-offs

In the area of sales
- Competitive information
- Sales cycle
- Market share

- Product differentiation
- Price resistance
- Paperwork
- Customer service and support

In the area of product development
- Development cycle
- Innovation
- Marketing focus
- Test marketing

In the area of personnel
- Turnover
- Absenteeism
- Morale
- "Buy-in"

In the area of image
- Relations with regulatory agencies
- Environmentalists' demands
- Public and press relations

If you have trouble listening to others, it's probably because you are too busy listening to yourself. We are all taught how to talk. As part of our sales training we are taught how to give our pitch. And we all have a lot of experience at planning and rehearsing what we are going to say next while the other person is speaking. The message we send to the customer by not listening attentively is "I don't think what you have to say is very important."

We are rarely ever taught how to listen. Yet all of us have the ability to be outstanding listeners. Let me illustrate with a personal story. I was down in Texas going through jet fighter pilot training. Before they let you blast off in one of those things, you have to go to ground school and learn the fuel system, the control systems, and so on. One day the instructor walked into the classroom and held up a large pin attached to a red ribbon. He asked, "Do you know what this is?" Of course, we had no idea what it was. Then he said: "This is the safety pin from the ejection seat. For the next hour I am going to lecture to you on how to eject and survive. Then, when we finish this lecture, we will all go out to the parade ground where we have an actual ejection seat mounted on a vertical railroad track. One at a time, each of you will strap into the seat, pull your visor down, raise the left arm rest, raise the right arm rest, then pull the trigger underneath the right arm rest. When you do that, a live 20-millimeter shell will explode under your you-know-what, and you will be shot 120 feet straight up in less than three seconds."

How well do you think we listened? Let me tell you—every person in that room could have given the lecture.

The most common mistake that people make about listening is to regard it as passive activity. Listening is not passive. It is an activity of the mind, not of the ear. It requires a major expenditure of intellectual energy. You have only one chance to accurately perceive and understand what is being communicated; you cannot rewind and replay. And unlike reading a book, you cannot go back and relisten to what you just heard.

Listen to this story:

> A businessman had just turned off the lights in the store when a man appeared and demanded money. The owner opened a cash register. The contents of the cash register were scooped up, and the man sped away. A member of the police force was notified promptly.

Now answer "True" or "False" to the following statements without rereading the story.

1. A man appeared after the owner had turned off his store lights.
2. The robber was a man.
3. The man did not demand money.

4. The man who opened the cash register was the owner.
5. The store owner scooped up the contents of the cash register and ran away.
6. Someone opened a cash register.
7. After the man who demanded money scooped up the contents of the cash register, he ran away.
8. Although the cash register contained money, the story does not state how much.

Most people believe they understand what they think you said, but I am not sure they realize that what they heard you say is not what you meant.

How to Hear What the Customer Says

Studies show that most people will forget 75 percent or more of what they hear in 24 hours or less. There are three tricks of the trade that will give you "20/20" hearing:

1. *A total tune-in.* You know in advance that you will be talking only 20 percent of the time and listening 80 percent of the time. And most of that 20 percent is asking questions. Your work at the CIA will let you prepare in advance a list of questions to ask. Therefore there is no need or reason to occupy your mind about what to say next. You will be able to totally tune in to what the customer is saying. Encourage the customer to talk by using verbal signals such as "Mm—hmmm" or "I see" or nonverbal signals such as nodding your head. This will further focus your mind on what the customer is saying and will send the message to the customer that what he or she is saying is very important.

2. *Take notes.* A short pencil is far superior to a long memory. Imagine that you have to give a detailed briefing of what the customer said to the president of your company. This accomplishes three things. It captures specific and de-

tailed information for your (or your management's) later review. It also forces you to concentrate more intensely on what the customer is saying. Lastly, when you say to the customer, "Do you mind if I take notes?" you send a very loud signal that says, "What you are going to say is very important to me."

3. *Confirm your understanding.* Confirming is accomplished by paraphrasing or summarizing what was said. This allows you to make sure that you got it right and forces you to listen better because you know you are going to restate what you heard. And (one more time) you are sending a signal that says, "What you are saying is so important that I want to be sure I get it right."

Nothing is more critical than getting the facts, the problems, and the priorities right. If we don't, we may propose solutions to problems that are low priority or nonexistent. You are guaranteed to lose if the customer says, "You don't understand." That will never happen if you confirm with phrases like these:

"So, if I understand you correctly. . . . Is that right?"
"What you've told me is that . . . . Am I correct?"
"Do I hear you saying that . . . ?"
"Putting that another way, would you say that . . . ?"
"Am I right in thinking that . . . ?"
"So what you're saying is . . ."
"Let me see if I understand what you just said about . . ."
"In other words, you're saying . . ."

Just in case you might think this subject of listening is too basic, may I observe that it is often the salespeople with the most knowledge and experience who talk the most and listen the least. Instead of talking about how valuable we are, we should learn how we can be of value. You can be of value if you can answer just one of the questions in Figure 7.4. But to answer any of those questions, you must first have good skills

If You Have Some Answers

YOU CAN MAKE AN EXECUTIVE CALL

1. How can you enhance your customer's CSFs?

2. How can your customer benefit from pending legislation?

3. Name one thing you could do in direct support of your customer's goals.

4. How can you help your customer lock in their largest customer?

5. How can you add value and differentiation to your customer's products or services?

6. What can you do to help solve the single biggest issue in the mind of the president?

7. How can you quickly produce a rewarding experience for a top executive?

8. How can your customer exploit the greatest weakness of their largest competitor?

9. What is your recommendation to help solve the biggest complaint or objections to your customer's products or services?

10. How can you reduce cost or increase sales?

Figure 7.4 To answer any of these questions, you must first have good skills in questioning and listening.

in questioning and listening. Business will get better when you do.

Are You Ready?

It's time for your first call on the Economic Decision Maker. Let's summarize where you stand and what you've done. You have

- Made a decision to call at the top (Chapter 1)
- Identified the Economic Decision Maker (Chapter 2)
- Solved the problem of the blocker at a lower level (Chapter 4)
- Got an appointment (Chapter 4)
- Spent ½ Day at the CIA (Chapter 5)
- Determined the behavioral style (Chapter 6)
- Prepared questions to ask (Chapter 7)

The purpose of your call is to

Question, Listen, and Learn

Buying is not a spectator sport. The customer or client has to be involved. If they are not talking, they will not be buying. Specifically you want to

- Confirm the Critical Success Factors. (You should have an informed opinion from your half day at the CIA.)
- Confirm the goals and objectives and get specifics. (You should know in general what these are from the annual report.) Please note that it is not appropriate to say to an executive of a public company "What are your goals?" You may get escorted to the door and be told to pick up a copy of the annual report on your way out. It is proof positive that you have not done your homework. Remember, the number one thing customers expect from a salesperson is

knowledge of their business, their industry, and their environment. Our questions should be directed to the specifics and details of the client's goals and objectives.
- Observe and confirm the behavioral style. (You should have made a good guess from talking on the phone or interviewing someone who knows the Economic Decision Maker.)
- Question to identify problems, needs, and wants—then quantify and determine consequences. (Start with the questions in this chapter.)
- Determine priorities by asking.

By way of contrast, take a look at the left side of Figure 7.5. This is the actual account planning process of a major Fortune 500 company. It is supported by an account planning manual that is 90 pages long and that doesn't include the forms to fill out. It is 100 percent vendor-oriented. Its major thrust is to decide what we think the customers should have, then try to sell it to them.

It's no wonder that a major study revealed that 56 percent of customers believe, "The salesperson seldom if ever knows what I need or want."

Our approach (on the right of Figure 7.5) is quite different. Find out what the customers want and give it to them.

Finally, there are three things you don't want to forget:

1. *The Key.* What key? The key to get back in. A preplanned question at the end of the call that will open the door for a return visit. For example, "May we get back to you with an executive presentation of the role we can play in helping you achieve your goal of _____?"
2. *The Blocker.* As we said earlier, don't leave the building without calling on the blocker for a detailed debriefing of the call. That builds trust and confidence and makes it easier next time.
3. *The Letter.* Mail a "thank you" letter to the executive before the sun goes down. Be sure to state in the letter

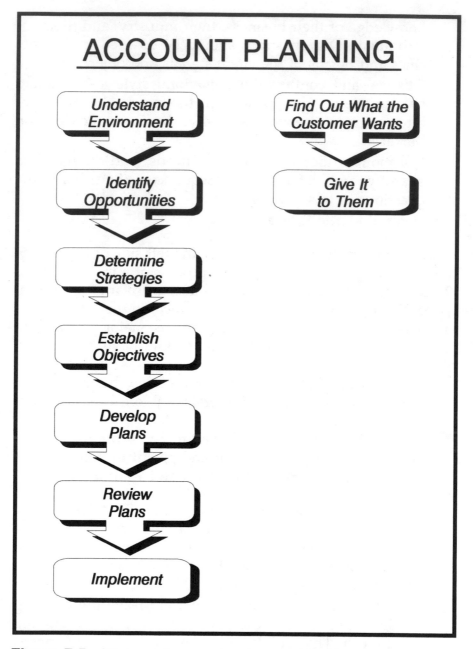

Figure 7.5   We can be vendor focused (left) or customer focused (right).

his or her agreement to a follow-up meeting for you to present your recommendations.

"But I can't remember all of that," you cry. I can't either. We need a "cheat sheet." Figure 7.6 is a shorthand script and cheat sheet to guide us through the call.

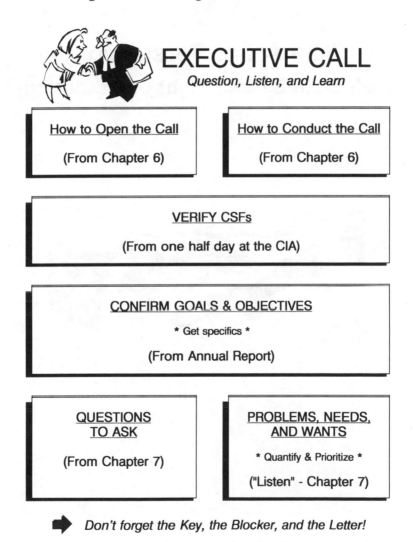

EXECUTIVE CALL
Question, Listen, and Learn

How to Open the Call	How to Conduct the Call
(From Chapter 6)	(From Chapter 6)

VERIFY CSFs

(From one half day at the CIA)

CONFIRM GOALS & OBJECTIVES

* Get specifics *

(From Annual Report)

QUESTIONS TO ASK	PROBLEMS, NEEDS, AND WANTS
(From Chapter 7)	* Quantify & Prioritize * ("Listen" - Chapter 7)

➡️ *Don't forget the Key, the Blocker, and the Letter!*

Figure 7.6 A shorthand script and "cheat sheet" to guide us through the call.

8
The Art of Persuasion
(Left Brain Selling; Right Brain Closing)

Whatever our profession, our business, our occupation, or our position, I would suggest that a key part of our job is to persuade other people to a course of action we would like them to take. The most significant and enduring effects on the human race throughout history have been accomplished with words and not with wars.

The answer to persuasion is not found in the latest fad or the newest three-dimensional model out of business school. Most of the great truths were discovered long ago. And so it is with the art of persuasion. The first and best book (personal opinion) on persuasion was written 2,400 years ago by Aristotle. In his book *Rhetoric*, Aristotle tells us the three things that are necessary to persuade another person to a course of action we would like them to take.

Scientific advances in more recent times have both confirmed and enhanced the wisdom of Aristotle. For example, it is now understood that certain functions are associated with the left brain, whereas other characteristics are associated with the right brain. Left brain thinking is generally characterized by logic, facts, and analytical reasoning. Right brain thinking is more concerned with feeling and emotion. We can use the wisdom of Aristotle and these discoveries to answer the following questions:

- Why people buy
- How people buy
- How to win
- How to lose

Aristotle's Answer

The first thing that Aristotle said is necessary to persuade another person is to appeal to their *logos*. That's a Greek word meaning *logic*. We must provide logical and factual reasons. But Aristotle said facts are not enough. If they were, then no one in America would smoke cigarettes and everyone who drives

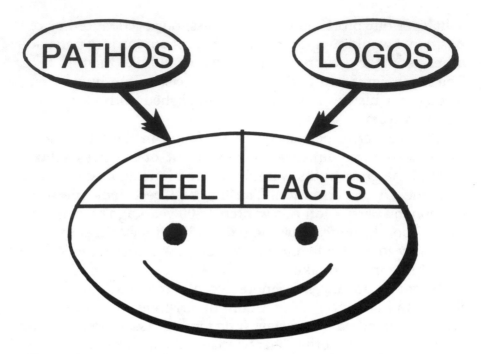

Figure 8.1   Aristotle said we must appeal to both the
logos (logic) and the *pathos* (emotion).

a car would always buckle up. But people continue to smoke,
and every day people die because they didn't wear a seat belt.
Aristotle said we must also appeal to their *pathos*—another
Greek word, meaning *emotion*.

Aristotle said all human behavior is a blend of the rational
and the irrational—the conscious and the unconscious.

We like to believe that our actions are rational and goal-
oriented. And they are—partly. But we are also driven by psychological needs of which we are largely unaware. We need to
feel

- Accepted
- Respected
- Productive
- Safe and secure

And we avoid situations that cause us to feel

- Anxious
- Threatened
- Depressed

or situations that cause us to look

- Incompetent
- Foolish
- Weak

Our decision-making process is summarized in Figure 8.2.

LEFT BRAIN

Facts & Logic

- Impact of the product or service on the business

- Tangible
  Measurable
  Quantifiable

Business Reasons

RIGHT BRAIN

Feelings & Emotion

- Fulfillment of a personal wish or desire

- Intangible
  Not measurable
  Not quantifiable

Personal Reasons

Figure 8.2   How we make decisions.

Let me tell you a story. A friend of mine bought a new Porsche. Because the price tag is four or five times greater than other vehicles with four tires and a steering wheel, I asked my friend, "Jim, why did you buy the Porsche?" Figure 8.3 summarizes his answer.

First Jim told me about the horsepower and engine characteristics. Then he told me how it will go from 0 to 60 in the blink of an eye. Finally, he told me about the great trade-in value. And so, in summary, he said, "I bought it because it's a good investment."

I didn't say it, but I was thinking to myself, "If it's such a great investment, why didn't you buy three?"

Then Jim asked, "Would you like to go for a ride in my Porsche?" I replied, "Sure." So we climbed in and lay down. I thought I was back in the cockpit of a fighter jet. Suddenly I felt the tremble and heard the roar as the engine came to life. Jim reached over, opened the glove compartment—and you wouldn't have believed these funny-looking gloves he put on his hands. Then in a cloud of dust and a screech of the tires we were off!

I looked over at my friend Jim. He had this big smile on his face. (I wish I could use the only phrase that really describes that smile.) I asked, "Jim, how do you feel?" He answered, "I feel 20 years younger." (This guy is 50 years old.) "I feel like Al Unser," he said and then continued, "You know, Dave, when I drive down the street in my Porsche, people turn and look at me. Nobody's looked at me in 20 years." Then under his breath I heard him whisper, *"It makes me feel good."*

PORSCHE

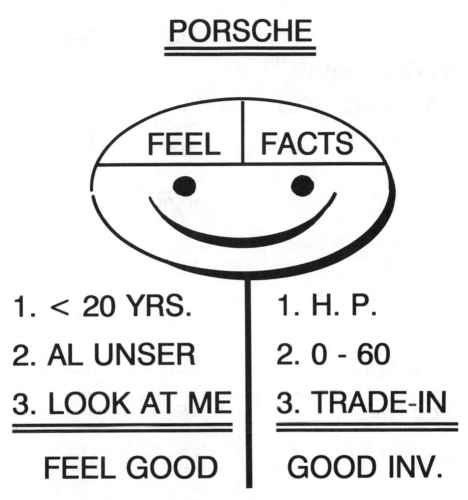

Figure 8.3   Why buy a Porsche?

Why did Jim buy the Porsche? Did he buy it because of the engine, the speed, and the trade-in-value? Or did he buy the Porsche because it made him feel good?

By the way, the president of Porsche has described the Porsche sales strategy by saying "A Porsche is not a car—a Porsche is the best-engineered executive toy in the world."

Let me tell you about my two watches. I will call them watch "X" and watch "Y". Take a look at Figure 8.4.

Which watch would you pick?

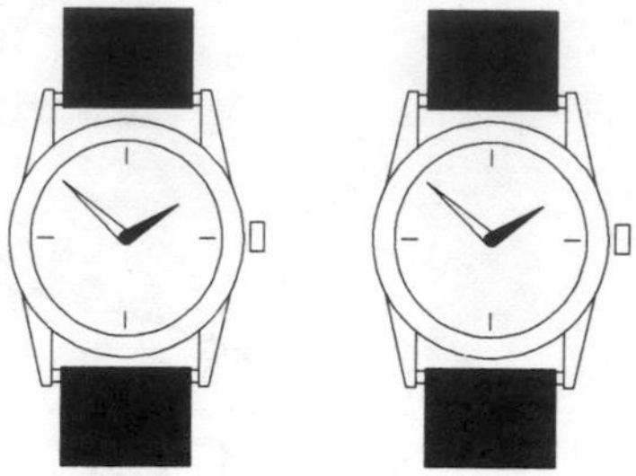

	"X"	"Y"
Accurate Time	YES	YES
Alarm Clock	YES	NO
Jogging Pacer	YES	NO
Stop Watch	YES	NO
Timer	YES	NO
Month	YES	NO
Date	YES	NO

Figure 8.4 Which watch do most people want?

Which watch has more functions and more features? If you were a purchasing agent, which would you think is clearly the superior watch?

Watch "X" is a Japanese watch encased in black plastic. I got it at the duty-free gift shop at the London airport. Price—$17.95.

Watch "Y" is an Omega encased in gold. I got it at the finest watch shop in Lucerne, Switzerland. Price—over $500. Which watch would you rather have? Be careful now. Watch "X" is the clear winner. It has more functions, more features, and is clearly the superior price performer. Yet most people want watch "Y".

Let's do a little left brain thinking about food. What is the logical and rational reason for eating? Answer: to provide nourishment and energy for the body. Now, let's go out to eat. We can go to restaurant "X" or restaurant "Y" (see Figure 8.5). Both have clean and wholesome food. No reservations are required at "X," but they are recommended for "Y." There is immediate seating at "X," but there is a wait time of 45 minutes to get a table at "Y." There is free parking at "X" but valet parking at "Y." The wait time to be served after you order is 7 minutes at "X" but 20 minutes at "Y" (on top of the 45 minutes required to get a table).

Let's say we order a New York steak. The price at "X" is $7.25. The price at "Y" is $23.95.

Restaurant "X" is Denney's. "Y" is the Coach and Six—an upscale restaurant in Atlanta, Georgia.

And now I ask you, why will people pay to park, wait in line, and pay lots of money for food that is no more wholesome than that which is available at a third of the cost? Yet the Coach and Six is often so packed that you can't get in it at any price without a reservation.

How about a little left brain thinking about automobiles. What is the purpose of a car? Answer: to provide transportation from point A to point B. How much does a car cost that will get you from point A to point B? If you are an average American, you paid over 60 percent more money than is necessary to completely fulfill the left brain's requirements for an automobile. Some pay 100, 200, even 300 percent more money than is necessary. I did so myself.

During my "Selling to the Top" seminars, I ask for a show of hands of those who have an American Express Card. Most hands go up. I then point out that there are other credit cards you can get for free. And even if you pay an annual charge,

Which restaurant would you pick?

	"X"	"Y"
Good Food	YES	YES
Clean	YES	YES
Reservations	NO	YES
Wait Time (Table)	NONE	45 MIN.
Parking Charge	NO	YES
Wait Time (Food)	7 MIN.	20 MIN.
N.Y. STEAK	$7.25	$23.95

Figure 8.5 Why is it that people will wait in line, pay to park, and pay three times as much for food that is no more wholesome?

the American Express annual fee is over 300 percent greater than the average fee for other cards. And that's just for the basic green card; you pay more for the gold, and still more for the platinum. Why do millions of Americans pay over 300 percent more than they have to?

Let's think for just a moment about our last major purchase—any product or service that cost more than $300. Here's the acid test. Could you have fulfilled your basic need with a less-expensive product or service?

The bottom line is simply this: People don't buy products or services. They buy how they perceive those products or services will make them feel. Furthermore, emotional decisions tend to be fast and final, whereas logical decisions tend to be slow and lack commitment.

Your client's right brain is saying

- Don't sell me clothes. Tell me how great I look.
- Don't sell me a house. Tell me about location and great neighbors.
- Don't sell me toys. Tell me about my happy children.
- Don't sell me a home computer. Tell me how I'll be "ahead of the pack."
- Don't sell me insurance. Give me peace of mind and love of family.
- Don't sell me food. Talk to me about good health (or a sizzling Kansas City steak).

Our tendency is not to buy what we need but to choose what we want, and wants are based on feelings.

If you are married, which means having made probably the biggest decision of your life, did you insist on an I.Q. test, a medical exam, and a financial statement before you said "I do"? Or were there other, less logical factors involved?

This tendency can even apply to the work we choose. I remember how shocked I was to learn the mortality rate of jet fighter pilots. But I chose to become one because I wanted to look like and feel like Steve Canyon.

The point we are making is well understood by Madison Avenue. Do you think their advertising would tend to appeal to your logic or to your emotions? The answer is easy to understand when we look at the five strongest buying motives known to humanity in Figure 8.6. As you can see, three out of five are based on feeling and emotion.

BUYING MOTIVES

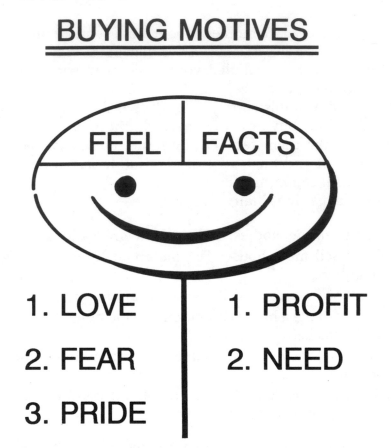

1. LOVE	1. PROFIT
2. FEAR	2. NEED
3. PRIDE	

Figure 8.6   Three of the five strongest buying motives are based on feeling.

J.P. Morgan, the great financier, once said, "A person usually has two reasons for doing something—one that sounds good and the real reason." And Dale Carnegie said, "When dealing with people remember that you are not dealing with creatures of logic but with creatures of emotion." Dr. Tom Stanley, in his book *Marketing to the Affluent*, writes, "Of the hundreds of millionaires I have interviewed, only one reported using totally objective evidence to evaluate sellers of investment services." And finally, listen to this quote from former Chief Justice Hughes of the U.S. Supreme Court: "Our level of decision making is 95 percent emotional."

There is a big distinction between a need and a want. A need is a necessity; a want is an inner urge that is strictly emotional. A customer or client may need something yet not want it (like a hearing aid). If they do not want it, they probably won't buy it. Conversely, they may want something (like the latest fad) but not need it. If the want is great enough, they will buy it, but only after they have justified it. That justification is often more accurately described as rationalization. And we are all world champions at converting rationalization to justification. It doesn't matter whether the subject is a pair of shoes, a face lift, or a Lear jet; if we want it enough, we will find a way to justify it—at least to ourselves.

This natural tendency of the human creature is summarized in Figure 8.7.

JUSTIFY ON FACTS
BUY ON FEELINGS

JUSTIFY WITH BUSINESS
REASONS
BUY FOR PERSONAL
REASONS

JUSTIFY WITH LOGIC
BUY ON EMOTION

Figure 8.7 The buying tendency of the human creature.

Why Do People Buy?

People buy for *their* reasons—not for ours. The problem is that our reasons tend to be left brain reasons. Just think of the content of your sales calls, your presentations, and your proposals.

You can hear the frustration of salespeople in the office bull pen. "My customer (client or prospect) is out of her ever-lovin' mind. Every month that passes without implementing my recommendation is costing her a jillion dollars in savings. It will eliminate five people, reduce inventory by 10 percent, and improve customer service. I don't understand."

You sure don't understand. You are transferring *your* buying reasons to the client. She isn't buying for your left brain reasons. She will buy for *her* reasons (right brain). Behind every logical need lurks an emotional want. If there is no emotional want, there will be no sale. Your mission is to show her how your product or service will also fulfill a personal want or wish, as shown in Figure 8.8.

If all of us did all our buying for left brain reasons, then all of us would

- Drive very basic cars
- Wear Japanese watches
- Eat at Denny's

PERSONAL REASONS	BUSINESS REASONS
• MORE POWER	• INCREASE SALES
• CONTROL OTHERS	• REDUCE COST
• SELF-ESTEEM	• ROI
• ENJOYMENT	• LESS RISK
• RECOGNITION	• BETTER QUALITY
• MORE LEISURE	• PRODUCTIVITY
• FAME & GLORY	• CONTROL
• TEAM PLAYER	• BETTER SERVICE
• RISK TAKER	• GOOD PRICE

Figure 8.8 People buy for *their* reasons (right brain), not for *our* reasons (left brain).

Let's look again at the hierarchy of human wants (Figure 8.9) and observe that three of the five wants are emotional yet all five respond to emotional buying reasons.

The left brain reasons (logic and justification) are important. You won't make the sale without the facts provided by the left brain. But the battery that fires the buying spark plug is more likely to be in the right brain. Yet most (sometimes all) of your focus as a salesperson is on the facts, the logic, and the business reasons.

Let's look at the other side of this coin. When you lose an account, a client, or a bid, are you given a left brain reason or a right brain reason for the loss? Almost always you are given a left brain reason. And by far the most common left brain

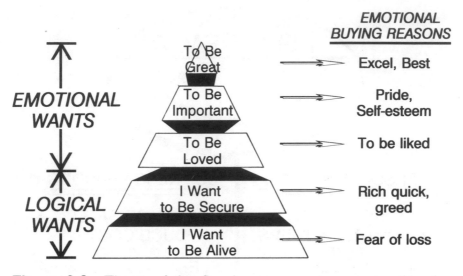

Figure 8.9 Three of the five human wants are emotional, yet all five *respond* to emotion.

reason given by the customer or client is price. Price as a reason (excuse) has business respectability: "You lost because your competitor's price was 15 percent less." But is that the real reason for the loss? Neil Rackham, in his book *Major Account Sales Strategy,* reports on a study of lost sales where the vendors were told they lost on price. Follow-up interviews revealed that in 64 percent of the cases price was *not* the reason for the loss.

Why do people buy?

To get some additional insight, let's combine what we've learned about the four types of behavioral styles with the wisdom of Aristotle and see where it leads us.

First we need a product. Listen to this story and see if you can guess what it is.

I grew up in the high country of northern Oregon.
I reached manhood in the heart of a mighty cedar tree on the south slope.

Then one day, a logger came by with his six-foot saw.
He cut me down, chained me to a flatbed truck, and shipped me to the mill far away, far away.

There I was sawed into short slats a quarter inch thick.
Then I was kiln dried and tinted to bring out my rich and
warm cedar color.

I was bedded down in a boxcar with thousands of my broth-
ers and sisters.
I heard the whistle, felt the rumble as the engine came to life.
We were off to the East in the morning sun.
The night came and the moon rose, and finally we arrived at
a factory in a valley in Pennsylvania.

A precision machine cut a groove down my middle, and laid a
length of lead in my new-cut bed.

I was covered with a blanket of glue, and a blank slat with an
empty groove was fitted on top of me.
My lead, now forever entombed in the center of my cedar, is
not lead at all.
It is graphite from Ceylon—now called Sri Lanka—off the
coast of India.
My graphite was mixed with clay from Mississippi; sprinkled
with chemicals and then extruded; cut to size; and dried and
baked at 1850°.
My body was ground to six sides, given three coats of lac-
quer, then embossed with your message on one of my sides.

My crowning glory was attached by a circle of brass.
It was made by mixing rapeseed oil from the Dutch East In-
dies with sulfur chloride, then adding rubber for binding and
cadmium sulfide to turn it red.

And now, at long last, my journey is over.
I have traveled many miles.
I come to you from many lands
and many hands.
I am the best that can be of what I am.
My wish and my dream is to find a home in your hand.

We see that one can tell a romantic (right brain) and fact-
filled (left brain) story about the simplest of products—a pencil.

Let us now consider why each of the four behavioral styles
from Chapter 6 would buy this pencil. The mind will tend to

JUSTIFY ON FACTS
(LEFT BRAIN)

Behavioral Style	Benefit	Feature
DRIVER	Lasts longer Reduces cost	High-density lead
ANALYTICAL	Most logical choice	Hexagonal design
AMIABLE	Proven & dependable	No moving parts
EXPRESSIVE	Promotional message	Embossing

Figure 8.10   Different facts for different folks.

BUY ON FEELINGS
(RIGHT BRAIN)

Behavioral Style	Benefit	Feature
DRIVER	Control distribution	Reorder system
ANALYTICAL	Viewed as best decision	Simple design
AMIABLE	User satisfaction	Never breaks
EXPRESSIVE	My name	Embossing

Figure 8.11   Different feelings for different beings.

justify it with a business reason, then purchase it for a personal reason. Figures 8.10 and 8.11 show how this process might look.

Aristotle's Third Requirement

That leads us to Aristotle's third requirement for persuading another person to a course of action we want him or her to take. He called it *ethos.*

Ethos is a Greek word that says people want to do business with people they like, trust, and have confidence in. They also want those people to be warm, friendly, and human. They do not want to do business with people they perceive to be cold, aloof, and arrogant.

Let me illustrate with a story and a study.

How many teachers have you had in your entire life—from kindergarten, grade school, middle school, high school, and college—including Boy Scouts, Girl Scouts, and religious instruction? And let's include presenters. How many people have stood up in front of you in your entire life? For purposes of discussion, would you agree to somewhere between 300 and 400? Then let me ask you this: Of those 300 to 400 people, how many were truly outstanding?

I've had the occasion to ask that question around the world. And whatever the country—whatever the language—the answer is always the same. Most people say three, four, or five, maybe six. Most people say, "I could count them on my fingers and have fingers left over."

Next question. Here is the president of a company. He's been president for 20 years. During that time, how many salespeople (bankers, brokers, insurance salespeople, and so on) do you think have called on him? Probably 300—maybe 400.

If you turned to him and asked, "Mr. President, of the 300 to 400 salespeople you've seen in the last 20 years, how many were truly outstanding?" what do you think he would say? My guess is he'd reply, "I could count them on my fingers and have fingers left over."

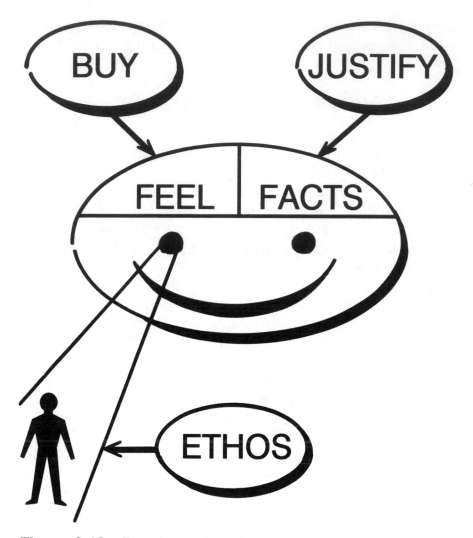

Figure 8.12 People tend to do business with people they trust (*ethos*).

What is it about the very few that makes them different?

We can get some insight to the answer to that question from a survey of 12,000 students that asked them to list the characteristics of the very few teachers they'd had whom they considered truly outstanding. Their answers are in Figure 8.13.

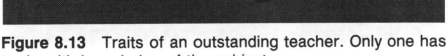

OUTSTANDING

Cooperative, Democratic
Kind, Considerate
Patient
Wide interests
Pleasant
Fair, Impartial
Sense of Humor
Good Disposition
Interest in Student Problems
Recognition, Praise
Flexible
Proficient in Subject

Figure 8.13 Traits of an outstanding teacher. Only one has to do with knowledge of the subject.

Now I ask you—of these characteristics, how many have to do with knowledge of the subject? One. Only one has to do with knowledge of the subject.

That was the good news. There's also bad news—characteristics of the worst teachers, listed in Figure 8.14. Again I ask you—how many have to do with explaining the subject itself? And again, the answer is only one.

WORST

Never Smiles
Sarcastic
"Flies Off the Handle"
Explanations Not Clear
Partial
Has Favorites
"Picks On" Some
Superior
Aloof
Overbearing
Not Friendly

Figure 8.14   Traits of the worst teachers. Only one has to do with explaining the subject.

So it is that our customers, our clients, and our prospects are sending to you and me a simple message that we do not hear in the complexity and the technicalities of the work we do: *Before I care how much you know, I want to know how much you care.*

Whether we like it or not, whether we agree or disagree, our customers, clients, and prospects are judging and measuring us by the truths shown in Figure 8.15.

We Are Measured

Not by what we are,
But by what we seem
to be.

Not by what we say,
But by how we are
heard.

Not by what we do,
But how we appear
to do it.

Figure 8.15   How we are judged and measured.

As Daniel Webster said, "The world is governed more by appearance than by realities."

At IBM when we surveyed customer satisfaction (and we did every year), we consistently found that the single greatest variable in overall satisfaction was the salesperson assigned to the account. Yet, sad to say, when we broke overall satisfaction down into the following component parts:

- Hardware
- Software
- Maintenance service
- Technical support
- Salesperson

the item that was consistently ranked the *lowest* in satisfaction was the salesperson—in spite of the fact that IBM had an intense one-year sales training program.

You may have guessed by now that the training program was almost 100 percent left brain–oriented.

The results were predictable. Here's some typical feedback from IBM's largest customers: "Reps [IBM sales representatives] need to improve their Business/Interpersonal relationship skills" and "We don't want a vendor, we want a relationship. If we treat you like a vendor, it's because you act like a vendor." A case study entitled "The Transformation of IBM," published by the Harvard Business School, quotes a major IBM customer as saying, "I feel the people issue has been IBM's most serious problem for some time." And in an interview for a trade magazine, IBM's chairman said that "the IBM of yesterday was a bit too reserved . . . . [it] wasn't as approachable as people would have liked." Customer satisfaction tumbled. In a multistate opinion survey, 32 percent of the customers said, "IBM is not responsive."

Additional insight comes from the results of a survey shown in Figure 8.16.

Win/Win Has Lost Its Meaning

An oft-quoted and oversimplified solution is to play "win/win." But like *motherhood* and *brotherhood,* these words have lost the intensity of their meaning through overuse. Let's review the consequences of the alternatives.

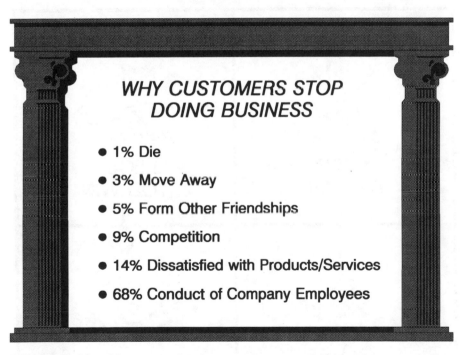

WHY CUSTOMERS STOP DOING BUSINESS

- 1% Die
- 3% Move Away
- 5% Form Other Friendships
- 9% Competition
- 14% Dissatisfied with Products/Services
- 68% Conduct of Company Employees

Figure 8.16   You are the messenger and the message.

I Win—You Lose

We can say and promise anything to get the business. Unfortunately, if you oversell, you will underdeliver. And so this strategy, even in moderation, will sooner or later deteriorate into I Lose/You Lose as shown in Figure 8.17. Customers will perceive that your agenda is not their agenda and that you do not have their best interests at heart. The bottom-line results of this strategy are dramatic and can be seen in Figure 8.18. Research by the consulting firm of Bain & Company showed

Figure 8.17   A trophy versus a ticking time bomb—the choice is yours.

Figure 8.18 Buyer's remorse becomes buyer's revenge.

that boosting customer retention by 2 percent has the same effect on profit as cutting costs by 10 percent.

Making quota at any price is like shooting yourself in the foot. The naive salesperson sees

- The buyer as an adversary
- The order as a prize
- Selling as a contest, with the customer as the enemy

The realities of life and business are just the opposite. If you are in the game for the long haul, then it is mandatory that you work toward having

- Long-term relationships
- Satisfied clients
- Good references

Remember what the customer said: "We don't want a vendor, we want a relationship."

Some of the worst account situations are those where sometime in the past another salesperson played the game of I Win/You Lose. The victim has never forgotten it and never will. Worse, he or she may now be the Dominant Influencer or the Economic Decision Maker. During my "Selling to the Top" seminars I ask salespeople, "How many of you have an account like that?" Eighty percent of the hands go up.

Could you have that kind of an account situation and not be aware of it? Of course, we all can. Some customers will never tell, but they will never forget, either. So the answer to the mystery at the XYZ Company may be an event that happened 20 years ago that you will never know about.

I Lose—You Win

This is where you make concessions in price, quality, service, support, and so on. The rationale is that the customer will be impressed and will reciprocate in the future by giving you additional business. The problem is one of perception. You give the buyer a false sense of reality, one that cannot be maintained indefinitely.

When you buy the business by giving away your product, services, or time, you set up the buyer to lose in the future by raising his or her expectations. No company is going to "give away" forever. When it's time for the devil to be paid, the message to your customer is "Now it's your turn to lose." The I Lose/You Win degenerates into Lose/Lose.

The bottom line is simply this: If it's not a Win/Win, then sooner or later the bubble bursts and the bomb explodes. You may not hear the explosion, but the result is a locked door and a lost key.

Our Most Important Asset

The most important asset over which you and I have control is our relationship with our customers and our clients. That asset is either appreciating or depreciating. The control is in our hands, and we will be rewarded accordingly.

The good news is that it's easier to differentiate yourself than your product, for two reasons:

1. No company can consistently maintain product superiority.
2. All products are racing toward "look alike."

For over a quarter of a century, IBM was the shining example of the growth company. Yet for most of its period of meteoric growth, its products were only adequate—not superior.

Here's the message: *If there's not much difference between your product or your service and those of your competitors, then there better be a big difference in the way you deal with people.* The more generic the product, the more important you become and the more likely it is that the decision will be based on you. If they don't like you, they won't buy from you.

How to Deal with People—Building Trust, Confidence, and Likability

Your customer or client will have five questions about you as an individual completely apart from your company and your products or service. They will never ask the questions directly, but nevertheless they will formulate an answer based on their perception of you. Their answers to these five questions will determine the relationship and will be absolutely key to your business success.

Are You Dependable and Reliable?

Do you

- Do what you say you are going to do?
- Do it when you say you are going to do it?
- Do it right the first time?
- Get it done on time?

Do you walk like you talk or, after all is said and done, is more usually said than is ever done? Your customer or client's perception of your dependability will increase commensurately with the number of occasions on which his or her expectations are confirmed by your actions. It is mandatory that your performance matches your promise.

Herein lies an opportunity for you to differentiate yourself from your competitors by doing more than you are paid to do and by giving better service than you are paid to give. One of the biggest criticisms of salespeople is their lack of responsiveness. That's opportunity knocking. When a customer or client asks you to do something, do it now—right now. Look at it this way. You're going to do it sometime anyway, so why not differentiate yourself and earn confidence and respect by doing it now. For example:

- Say you'll have it done by Friday, then do it before the sun goes down today.
- Promise delivery on the 30th, but ship on the 10th.

What a breath of fresh air you will be to your customer or client. You will be perceived as a "breed apart."

If you run into trouble, give your customers a lack-of-progress report. It's almost as good as a progress report. Let them know what you've done, where you stand, and your game plan. Don't leave them twisting in the wind. Silence ain't golden— it's deadly. It's always better to over-communicate.

Are You Candid?

Does your customer or client see you as a salesperson giving a pitch or as a human being who tells it like it is. To be a partner and not a peddler, you must tell both the pros and the cons— the advantages and the disadvantages. Why not? The customer will do his or her homework and identify the soft spots in your proposal anyway. So again, it's an opportunity to differentiate yourself by letting him or her hear about the limitations from you first. Moreover, you may be able to frame those limitations in a better context. To discuss both sides is to do the unexpected. You will be seen as different and better. The more candid you are about the limitations of your product or service, the more credibility you will have over your competitors, because they won't and don't.

Are You Competent?

Your customer or client will be making judgments about you in such areas as

- Your technical or professional knowledge
- Your skill or experience
- The quality of your judgment
- The wisdom of your recommendations

If left to chance, your customer could easily come to the subjective conclusions that are not in your best interests. The quickest and best way to be perceived as highly competent is through the use of *proof sources*. Proof sources are other people who will testify to your competence. In sales talk, these are *references*. To the extent that the references are in the same industry or profession, are at an executive level, and are known and respected by your customer, you will get an immediate and unquestioned stamp of approval.

You can further enhance your image of competence by discussing relevant subjects your customer is likely to know about and understand. This is the technique to be used if you are new and have not yet developed proof sources. Examples of subjects might be

- Industry studies or surveys
- Quotes of recognized experts
- New developments and trends
- Pending legislation

Your customer's perception of your credibility increases directly with the number of your facts and observations that they know to be true.

Are You Customer Focused?

What is your intent? Do you have a hidden agenda? Do you have my best interests at heart? When push comes to shove, will you push your product with the commission bonus or recommend what's right for me?

We have already discussed one technique that will create a positive image of being customer focused: discussing both the pros and cons of your product or service. The more a salesperson talks about limitations, the more the client will perceive that the salesperson has his or her best interests at heart.

Another technique to create a positive, customer-focused image is to use what we learned at the CIA—talking their talk.

Talk about *their* problems, *their* concerns, *their* goals, *their* objectives, *their* strategy. What we choose to talk about tells clients or customers what we are interested in. To the extent that we talk about them, we demonstrate our interest in them.

Do I Like You?

People tend to do business with people they like. Your customers will like you if they believe you are sincerely interested in them.

The more impressed we are by *other* people's qualities and abilities, the more impressed *they* are with *our* qualities and abilities. The surest way to get other people interested in us is to be interested in them. If we want others to believe in us, the surest way is to believe in them. If we want people to like us, the surest way is to like them. If you want a friend, as Emerson said, you must first *be* a friend.

Emerson also said, "Every man is my superior in some way." Our mission is to find the ways.

We all have a need for high self-esteem. Whatever we do to increase the self-esteem of others will increase the quality of our human relations.

We cannot raise the self-esteem of another person without raising our own. If we make people sincerely feel good about themselves, it makes us feel good about ourselves.

The best way to say "I like you" is by giving honest and sincere appreciation. Dr. John Dewey, the philosopher, said that "the deepest urge in human nature is the desire to be important." Freud called it the desire to be great. And William James said, "The deepest principle in human nature is the craving to be appreciated."

And have you heard these heavy words by William Penn:

Any good that I can do
Any kindness I can show
To any human being

Let me do it now . . .
For I shall not pass this way again.

Let me tell you the story of Joe Girard. He was a car sales-man. Now I realize that you may not identify with car salesmen, but wait a minute. Joe Girard was special—so special that he's in the *Guinness Book of World Records.* For 11 consecutive years, Joe Girard was the number one car salesman in the United States. How long does it take to buy a car—from the time you arrive, look them over, kick the tires, test drive, negotiate, agree on trade-in, complete all the paperwork—maybe two to three hours or half a day? How many cars a day would you think the number one car salesman in the United States would have sold?

Joe Girard averaged selling five cars a day for 11 consecutive years. How did he do it? Joe had a name-and-address file of 13,000 people. Every month 13,000 people received in the mail a card in a plain envelope from him that bore this simple mes-sage: "I like you.—Joe Girard."

People would wait in line to buy a car from Joe Girard.

Speaking of cars, remember that car I paid 200 percent more money for than I needed to for basic transportation? When I took it in for its first checkup, the total bill was only $19.75. Never in my life had I received such a modest bill after putting a car in the shop. The service manager who took care of me was named Vickey Land. Two days later I received in the mail a hand-addressed envelope. Inside was a plain card with four words: "Thanks for your business"—signed by Vickey Land. Now, I've been taking cars in for maintenance for many years and no one has ever even said thank you for your business, let alone written me a personal note for a bill of only $19.75. Guess who gets all my car business? Vickey Land.

So let's say it again. It's easier to differentiate yourself than it is your product or service.

Here's another one that works wonders. Other than your family, who do you ever get a birthday card from?

How about a new twist on an old idea? How about a birthday card to your client on the anniversary of the first order, the first installation, the completion of your first engagement, and so on. The note would say, "It was exactly one year ago that . . . ." I betcha your competitors don't do that.

Harvey Mackay, who wrote the book *Swim with the Sharks*, tells the stories of

- The avid fisherman (customer) who received an article on salmon fishing in Scotland
- The opera buff who gets the season program for Carnegie Hall and Lincoln Center
- The Michigan alumnus who is mailed the program for the Rose Bowl

And from the book *Marketing to the Affluent* by Dr. Tom Stanley, we read the story of the stockbroker in New York who subscribed to the Sunday newspaper of Seattle, Washington, because that was the hometown of a New York executive whose business he wanted. Once a week the executive received a clipping of a newsworthy item about his hometown. The stockbroker got the business.

How to Build a Relationship

It's easy. Just do three things:

1. Smile
2. Call people by their name and pay them sincere compliments
3. Stop talking and start listening

That's a three-second summary of the best-selling book ever written on the subject—*How to Win Friends and Influence People* by Dale Carnegie.

We said earlier that your customers or clients will like you if they believe you are sincerely interested in them. The best way to demonstrate your interest is not with words but with action, as outlined in Figure 8.19.

We said earlier that it is not a problem to go over the head of someone and call at the top if that someone trusts and has

BUILD A RELATIONSHIP

Subject	Answer	Action
Birthday		Birthday Card
Names of Spouse and Children		Ask About, Show Interest
Hobbies and Special Interest		Clipping Service Related Gift
Dates of Major Events		Card, Cross Pen, Potted Plant
Favorite Subjects		Learn About, Ask About, Talk About
Areas of Strength		Pay Sincere Compliment
Personal Goals		Support, Encourage, Assist
Favorite Foods		Specialty Restaurant
Alma Mater		Favorite Sport Schedule

Figure 8.19   Say "I like you" by action, not words.

confidence in you. A proven way to develop that trust and confidence is summarized in Figure 8.20.

As we enhance the quality and the value of our relationship, amazing things can happen to the decision process. Let's consider an example of the most common technique of making a product or service decision. Figure 8.21 is an example of the decision matrix where the various vendors are ranked and rated against the selection criteria.

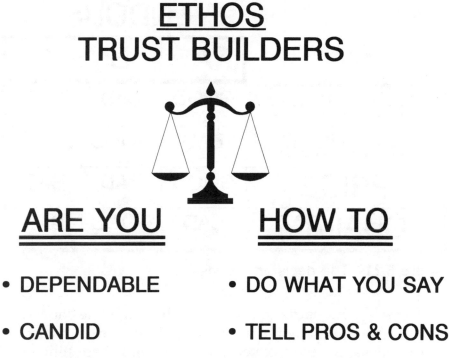

ETHOS
TRUST BUILDERS

ARE YOU

- DEPENDABLE

- CANDID

- COMPETENCE

- CUSTOMER
  FOCUSED

- LIKEABLE

HOW TO

- DO WHAT YOU SAY

- TELL PROS & CONS

- PROOF SOURCES

- TALK THEIR TALK

- SHOW INTEREST

Figure 8.20   How to enhance your most important asset.

How to Select a Vendor

VENDORS

	A	B	C
FEATURES	GOOD	BAD	GOOD
SERVICE	BAD	GOOD	GOOD
PRICE	GOOD	BAD	BAD
QUALITY	BAD	GOOD	BAD

Figure 8.21   The decision process.

The selection matrix can be as simple as the one shown, or it can be pages in length with numbers in the boxes carried to four decimals. Let me ask you this question: If I am filling out that matrix, can I make it come out any way I want it to? I sure can. And your client can too.

So what masquerades as technical analysis is actually highly judgmental and significantly influenced by whom I want to do business with. The human mind has the unique ability of being able to justify anything.

We can summarize the decision process in Figure 8.22.

Human beings tend to justify on facts, buy on feelings, and do business with people they like, trust, and have confidence

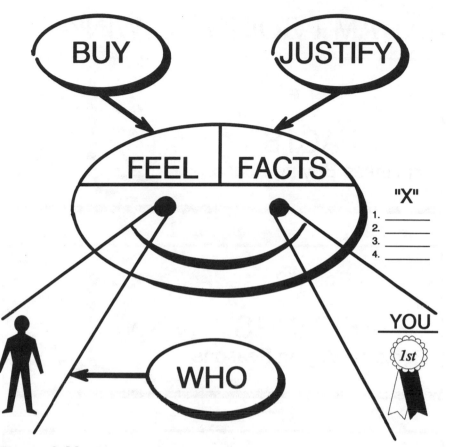

Figure 8.22   How to win.

in. You don't have to be outstanding to win. Most of your competitor's marketing strategy is based on only one of these three—that is, the facts. So if you only do a reasonable job of addressing the personal buying reason and building a relationship, you are likely to win the ribbon. The customer's focus will not be on the functions, features, bells and whistles of "X." The customer's focus will be on you. You will win.

Don't let yourself get caught in the trap that's shown in Figure 8.23. Here we see that you have the facts and the business buying reason on your side. However, brand "X" has done a better job of appealing to feelings and personal buying reasons. The tie breaker is *ethos.* The customer or client likes, trusts, and

AM I GOING TO WIN?

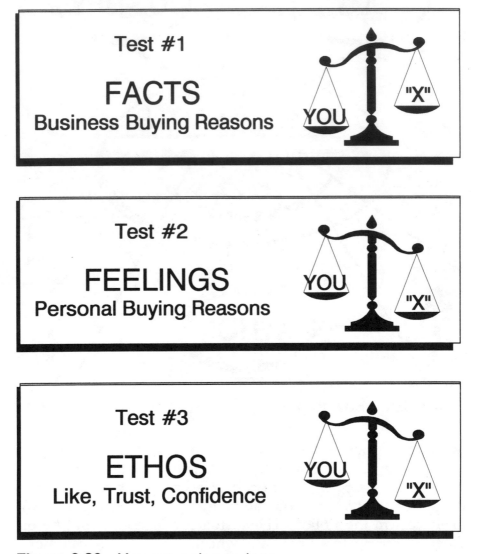

Figure 8.23 You are going to lose.

has more confidence in "X" than you. You are going to lose. The human mind can rationalize anything from burning witches at the stake to buying brand "X." Just because you have the most bells and the loudest whistles doesn't mean you are going to win. So follow the wisdom of Aristotle that has stood the test of time for 2400 years.

Why Call at the Top

In the first chapter we looked at the reasons for calling at the top. But I said there was another reason yet to come. Here it is. If you call at the bottom or the middle, you are relying on another party to communicate your message to the (Economic) Decision Maker. That message will almost certainly be stripped of everything except the facts (left brain). So when the decision maker hears your story from a third party, they hear only one of the three things that Aristotle said is necessary to persuade another person—the left brain reasons. You will almost surely lose. The only way you can appeal to the left brain, the right brain, and to *ethos* is to do it yourself, in person.

9
Presenting the Answer
(How to Differentiate Yourself from Your Competitor)

PRESENTING
THE
ANSWER

The purpose of your first call was to question, listen, and learn. If you did your homework and followed instructions, you have

1. Verified the Critical Success Factors
2. Confirmed the customer's goals and objectives and obtained specifics and details where they relate to your product or service
3. Prioritized specific wants, needs, and problems
4. Identified barriers to success
5. Verified through personal observation the behavioral style of the executive
6. Identified business buying reasons and personal buying reasons
7. Got agreement on a follow-up meeting

Figure 9.1 is a planning guide and work sheet for your second call. You can now fill in the boxes with the confirmed and verified answers for

- Critical Success Factors
- Customer's goals and objectives
- Business buying reasons (from Chapter 6)
- Personal buying reasons (from Chapter 6)
- Wants, needs, and problems

Your mission now is to structure our recommendations so that they

1. Relate to specific wants, needs, or problems of the customer
2. Are acknowledged as high priority
3. Tie to the customer's goals, objectives, and Critical Success Factors
4. Overcome obstacles

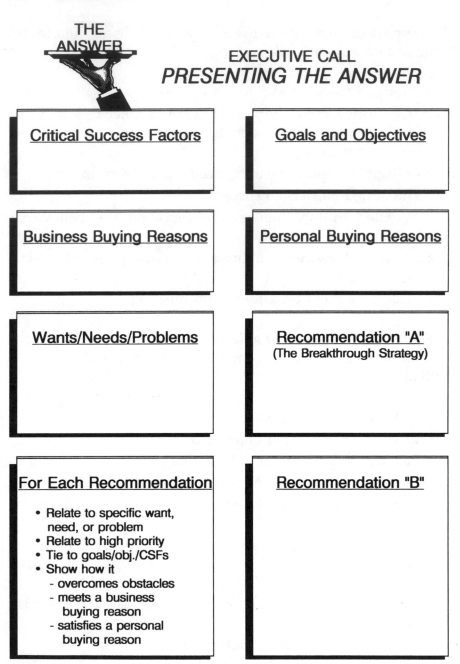

Figure 9.1 Executive call planning guide.

Customer Concerns	*Your Uniqueness*	*Prove It*
Quality Productivity Cost Control Sales Versatility Reliability Convenience Morale Security Etc.		

Figure 9.2   You need to relate your uniqueness to the concerns of the customer/client.

5. Meet a business buying reason
6. Satisfy a personal buying reason

Simply put, what customer problem does your product or service solve?

You must be able to relate the uniqueness of your product or service to the concerns of the customer or client. A simple matrix like Figure 9.2 will help you keep your eye on the customer's target.

Before you start filling in the unique column with things like "faster," "better," and "cheaper," let's do a little exercise. Take out a piece of paper and draw a vertical line down the center. On one side list the strengths and advantages of your product or service. On the other side, list what your top three competitors would say are their strengths and advantages. Now cross out like items on both sides of the line and see what you have left. You may not be as unique as you thought you were. Here's the problem from the customer's point of view: You may be the fourth guy or gal today who has talked about your "guarantee" as if you had the only guarantee in town—when, in fact, every supplier says that they guarantee their product or service.

So what can you do to differentiate yourself from your competitors? Here are six techniques that are proven winners with top executives.

Use the Breakthrough Strategy

The Breakthrough Strategy quickly produces a rewarding experience for a top executive as a direct result of your intervention.

Its greatest disciple, the man who coined the phrase and wrote the book (*The Breakthrough Strategy*), is Robert H. Schaffer. Bob Schaffer is a consultant's consultant. He runs a school to train would-be consultants how to be consultants, and his book documents the dramatic results of this strategy using actual cases.

The Breakthrough Strategy employs a startlingly simple logic that absolutely reverses the conventional wisdom of long-range planning and the search for the ultimate answer. It says that in any organization, at any moment in time, given the shortcomings of people, systems, methods, and equipment, there is always something that can be done right now to produce dramatic results.

Bob Schaffer gives five guidelines for selecting a goal for the Breakthrough Strategy:

1. It needs to be something that is not just important, but urgent—something that is recognized as vital and necessary now.
2. It must produce short-term results—not in months or years but in days or weeks. Business goals are often so big, so complex, and stretched so far out in the future that either you lose your way or the goal changes before you get there. You want to focus not on the total picture with its discouraging complexity but on finding a subgoal that can be accomplished quickly. This can be extracted from a large long-term goal in a number of ways, perhaps by focusing on one plant, one branch, or one department. Or the target might be one line of business, one class of customers, or even one large customer.
3. It should produce measurable, bottom-line results. If the subject is quality improvement, then the goal must be an actual reduction of defects or an actual increase in yields. If the subject is productivity, then the goal should be dollars saved or more units produced with the same resources.
4. It should be something that people are ready, willing, and able to do. People can be supporters or saboteurs of a project. We want the participants to say, "It's about time we did this." A person's readiness does not always coincide with the cold logic of a technologist, but it makes for a lot more enthusiasm.
5. The goal should be achievable with available resources and authority so that those who are carrying out the project can commit themselves—without hedged bets and escape clauses—to producing success.

Listen for Right Brain Opportunities

Your natural instinct will be to apply left brain thinking to the Breakthrough Strategy—that is, to apply features or characteristics of your product or service to the high-priority wants, needs, or problems of the customer. And that is exactly as it should be. But you can really ring the executive's bell if you listen for right brain opportunity. As previously discussed, the right brain is the home base of feelings and emotions, but it is also the center of creative thinking.

Here are some examples of right brain creative answers to customer situations that can have far greater impact than any product solution:

- In the first call it became clear that this was a mature industry with little or no growth in the United States. The executive was preoccupied with opening up new markets in Europe, but the company has no experience in overseas marketing.

  Your company has been doing business in Europe for many years. As it turns out, your country manager in Germany will be in the United States next month. Why not arrange for him to meet with your customer for a discussion of the dos and don'ts of marketing in Europe? That meeting could be worth tens of thousands of dollars to your customer, and it costs neither of you anything.

- In the first call the customer revealed, as a result of your questioning, the serious nature of a labor grievance situation.

  Your company has an experienced labor negotiator. Why not volunteer her services for consultation? You could be directly responsible for avoiding a shutdown.

- Your customer is considering a major change from direct sales to dealer sales.

  Your company is very experienced in dealer sales. What about a 90-day executive swap? You loan them a sales manager experienced in the dealer channel. They loan your company a manager experienced in an area of interest to your executives. Your idea can result in a smooth transition to dealer sales for your customer.

- From your half day at the CIA, you learn that your executive has been appointed chairperson of a fund-raising program for the local symphony. In the first call it became clear that it's very important to your executive that the program be successful.

  In your company there is an executive who headed a fund-raiser for the local art museum. You can bring them together, and your customer can avoid the mistakes others have made.

Salespeople rarely use—in fact, are largely unaware of—the resources within their own company that can have value to their customers at little or no cost.

The Breakthrough Strategy, whether left brain or right brain, is a unique approach that is outside the conventional wisdom of sales training. It provides another opportunity to differentiate yourself from your competitor and establish a long-term relationship that puts you above the crowd.

Tom Peters, one of the best known business authors and speakers in the world, said of the Breakthrough Strategy, "I am convinced that a well–thought out small-win approach is the premiere path to effective strategy implementation. . . ."

Use a Least-Risk Strategy

As we said earlier, the relative importance of price tends to decrease as you go up the organization. The man or woman at the top is more likely to be interested in the probability of success and the risk of failure. He or she realizes that the cheapest product or service becomes the most expensive if it does not do what it was bought to do.

Your competitors will be talking about their products' functions and features. You can be talking about experiences, training, testing, competence, credibility, and a pattern of proven success. It's the political equivalent of trust and character. When you do talk about the functions and features of your product or service, you can put it in the context of how they relate to least risk.

Three years ago I had major surgery. I was told it was my only chance and it had to be done immediately. Do you think I said, "Who is the cheapest surgeon?" Absolutely not. In fact, I asked for the most expensive. But I didn't phrase it that way. What I actually said was, "Who's the best?" Price was not a factor. I wanted the least risk.

The bigger the deal and the more there is at stake, the more likely it is that your executive will be receptive to a least-risk strategy.

When I was selling computers, I found that the FUD factor had a profound effect on top executives. FUD stands for Fear, Uncertainty, and Doubt. I built a clipping file of stories that documented disasters (even bankruptcies) as a result of a bad (spell that "low-cost") computer decision. That always got their attention and put price in perspective; it became less of a factor. Least risk became the dominant consideration. If you are selling least risk, you'll probably have the only game in town.

Sell a Business Philosophy

Your competitors are "pitching" the most bells and the loudest whistles on their product or service. As I said in Chapter 1, the relative importance of bells and whistles decreases as you go up the organization. In fact, a good way to get sent downstairs is to pitch the nitty-gritty details to top executives. Evaluating the pros, the cons, and the value of the details is the job of the folks downstairs—not the executives upstairs.

What will get the interest of the executives is a presentation and discussion of a business philosophy. This is a subject that's on their turf in a language they understand. For example:

- "Our business philosophy is to be the dominant expert in (your) industry."
- "Our business philosophy is to be the technology leader."
- "Our business philosophy is to provide one-stop shopping."
- "Our business philosophy is to provide for growth through upgrades rather than major replacements."
- "Our business philosophy is to provide the optimum balance between price and performance."
- "Our business philosophy is to tailor our products to the customer's needs."

Once you have established your business philosophy, you can talk about the value of that philosophy and what it means to the customer or client. You can then frame your unique features within the context of your business philosophy. By doing that, the features become the proof that supports it. Executives are more inclined to buy into a business philosophy than they are to buy a bell or whistle.

Every company has a business philosophy, whether they know it or not. Just ask some of your best clients why they do business with you. Their answer will be your business philosophy. Now if you will just sharpen it, fine-tune it, and enhance it, you will have a business philosophy that is also a marketing tool. I'll betcha that business will get better because you will have better defined your business.

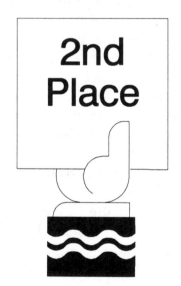

Sell First Choice for Second Place

The realities are that most prospects already have a supplier for most products and services. The idea that you could make a couple of sales calls and destroy an existing vendor's relationship that may have endured for several years is somewhat unrealistic, to say the least.

But here's an idea that is not unrealistic. Suppose that during your executive call, you acknowledge the existence of a satisfactory arrangement between your customer and their existing supplier. Furthermore, you make it clear that you do not expect them, and will not ask them, to change vendors. That's an immediate relief to the executive, and you will almost always notice a change in the atmosphere as he or she realizes that defending or rationalizing the existing supplier won't be necessary. The executive's guard comes down.

Explain that your objective is to be the first choice for second place as his or her supplier. You then proceed to present the business and personal reasons for you to be in second place. Do not ask then to buy anything. And do not "knock," criticize, or belittle the present supplier in any way. All you ask is an understanding and agreement that what you have to offer is attractive enough for you to be in second place. The executive does not have to make any decision, any commitment, or spend any money.

What a refreshing change you will be from other vendors who badmouth the existing supplier and ask the prospect to throw the rascals out and give them all the business. They are asking for a revolution; you are suggesting evolution.

Suppose you do this for dozens of prospects. Suppose you also follow this up with periodic mailings, newsletters, or flyers that are focused on your strategy of being first choice for second place.

The reality is that every year in every industry there is a change in some percent of the vendors. Even the best of vendors have their fair share of unhappy, dissatisfied, and "ticked-off" customers. If you have established yourself as the first choice for second place, then you will get some percent of this business. It's a numbers game. If you are number two in enough lines, it's just a matter of time until you become number one in some of them.

The ESS (Executive Service and Support) Review answers the question "What have you done for me lately?" If the nature of your product or service involves ongoing support and servicing of the account, an ESS Review is a powerful marketing tool that can effectively differentiate you from your competitor at the executive level.

Top executives are rarely aware of the total support and service they receive from suppliers. Even at lower levels the service is often distributed among several people or multiple departments. The result is that no single person is aware of your total support and service over the last year.

If you have never met the top executive, an ESS Review is an effective way to open the door to the executive suite. And what better way to start a relationship than to summarize all the things you have done for him or her over the last 12 months?

In Figure 9.3 we see an example of an ESS Review letter you can use to set up the review meeting with your executive. This is the same letter we used to open the door for our first call on Mr./Ms. Big back in Chapter 4. We can see that the subject of the letter is an Executive Service and Support (ESS) Review and that it answers these questions:

Dear Mr./Ms. Executive:

We value our partnership with __(customer or client name)__. It is our objective to provide value and solutions to your business issues. In doing so we assume total accountability for our products, our service, and our support. In order that we may evaluate our effectiveness, it is our practice to meet with our key customers (clients) for an Executive Service and Support Review.

This is not a sales presentation. Its purpose is to

- Say "Thank you" for your business
- Review a summary of our activities with your company over the past year and the results achieved
- Invite your feedback on the quality and value of our products (or service or support)
- Listen to your suggestions as to how we might serve you better
- Present our planned activities for the coming year and confirm that they are aligned with your business goals and priorities

It has been our experience that these reviews are mutually beneficial in retaining and enhancing both of our competitive positions in the marketplace.

Mr./Ms. __(executive from your company)__, our __(title)__, and I are looking forward to meeting you. You might wish to invite other members of your management team to join us. We expect that the meeting would last approximately 30 minutes.

I will call you on __(date)__ to arrange for a convenient date.

Sincerely, etc.

Figure 9.3 Example of an ESS Review letter.

- Why?
- What (purpose)?
- Who?
- How long?

Read the list of five items in the letter carefully. Doesn't that sound like motherhood, brotherhood, and apple pie? Your competitor is talking about features, functions, speeds, and feeds to the folks downstairs. What a study in contrast. What a way to differentiate yourself.

You will note that the letter says that this is not a sales presentation. That's a relief to the executive and elevates the meeting to a discussion of mutual interest among business people. But read again the fifth item under the purpose of the meeting. Bingo! If your "planned activities" are presented from the customer's point of view to answer the question "What's in it for me (the customer)?" it won't sound like or be taken as a sales pitch.

And if you're into customer service, you'll be amazed at what an ESS Review will do for customer satisfaction. Remember this rule: "The degree of management involvement will determine the level of management satisfaction."

Let's talk about our job as salespeople. I would like to suggest to you that our job is to persuade other people to a course of action we would like them to take.

I would like to recommend that when your time comes to persuade others, you should stand up and give a presentation using visual aids—as opposed to just talking across a desk. I say that because in a study done at the University of Minnesota it was revealed that if you stand up and give a presentation using visual aids, your audience, your client, or your prospect is 43 *percent more likely to be persuaded.*

But there's more. A bombshell came out of that study—unexpected and unanticipated by anybody: If you stand up and give a presentation, your client will be willing to pay *26 percent more money* for the same service.

There's more smoking-gun evidence. Let's go to the Wharton School of Business at the University of Pennsylvania. A controlled study was done using a presentation to try to persuade people to invest their money in a new business.

In that study, Group A told their story sitting down, talking across the table. When it was all over, 58 percent of targeted participants said, "I will sign up for that business proposition." Group B used the same facts, numbers, and statistics. Everything was identical except that the presenter stood up and used visual aids. Now, not 58 percent but 79 percent said, "I will sign up for that business proposition."

Moreover, the presenter who stood up and used visual aids was perceived by the audience as being

- More professional
- More persuasive
- More credible
- More interesting
- Better prepared

It's important to use visual aids. Here's another reason why. Studies show that without visual aids your client or prospect will forget 75 percent or more of what you say in 24 hours or less.

And there are yet more significant fringe benefits to giving a presentation using visual aids:

- Learning is improved up to 200 percent (from a study at the University of Wisconsin)
- Retention is improved up to 38 percent (from studies at Harvard and Columbia)
- Time required to explain complex subjects is reduced by 25 to 40 percent (from a study at the Wharton School of Business)

The critical message is this: In the minds of your clients, the quality of your presentation is a mirror image of the quality of

- Your company
- Your product
- Your service
- Your support
- Your people

We spend years in school and in training, learning and fine-tuning the skills of our profession, yet we spend little time learning the skills to communicate. But brilliance without the ability to communicate is worth as little today as it was in the days of Pericles.

It is a rare situation where one can have a successful and rewarding career communicating only with computers. As our businesses become more complex, the ability to communicate in concise terms becomes more important and more critical to our careers. Presentations come with the territory.

Research by the American Society for Training and Development concluded that "the only thing that ranks above communication skills as a factor in work place success is job knowledge."

So if you're looking for a horse to ride to get ahead, just become a good presenter. Notice I didn't say "excellent"—nor did I say "outstanding." Just become *good*—because the rest of the world is so terrible. You will do well if you just do "good" what most do so poorly. If you're not interested for yourself, think of your children—don't they deserve wealthy parents?

Please do not accept the myth that good speakers and presenters are born, not made. Lies—all lies. Speaking and presenting are skills that we learn through desire, effort, and practice. As with any other learned skill, some are better at it than others. But wherever you are on the scale today, I promise you that you can be three times better tomorrow.

People say to me, "Well, when the day comes that I have to stand up in front of 20, 50, or a few hundred people, I will prepare a presentation and make some visual aids. But most of my activity in persuading other people is one on one."

May I communicate to you the single most effective technique I have ever found for winning: the one-on-one stand-up presentation with him or her alone with me in my conference room or theirs. I know it sounds silly to give a stand-up presentation to one person, but the psychological impact is overpowering. Here's why.

You Will Be a Breed Apart

Most people have never in their lives had anyone give them a one-on-one stand-up presentation. The unspoken message you send to your prospect by doing so is this: "I'm putting you on a pedestal. I'm making you king or queen for a day. Your decision concerning my product or service is so important to me and my firm that I've organized and formalized my story. You deserve the best I've got to give. I believe that my service is so good and so aligned with your goals and your objectives that if I can effectively communicate your importance and my conviction, then I believe we will do business together."

The power of this unspoken message, as demonstrated by your actions, is overwhelming. Your competitors will not have a chance. They will do what everybody else does—that is, follow the course of least resistance and talk across the desk. What a study in contrast. You will have differentiated yourself from your competitor in a dramatic way. In the words of the stockbroker, you will be a "breed apart."

More Business—Less Effort—Less Time

As we discussed earlier, there are an average of five decision makers in a major services decision and seven in a major product decision. That means if you are doing your job, then you will need to call on five to seven people, and tell your story five to seven times.

That's going to take a lot of time. Now the only thing we all have the same amount of is time—but one of the biggest differences among us is how we use it.

Suppose, for example, I use the Fast-Track strategy and say, "Mr. or Ms. Decision Maker, I would like to have the opportunity to give a formal presentation to you and the other people involved in this decision." What I am doing is using a formal presentation as the catalyst to get all the decision makers together so that I can present my story one time professionally instead of five or seven times unprofessionally.

Charge a Higher Price

The professionalism you exhibit by giving a presentation will tend to eliminate (or at least minimize) requests for concessions or special contractual arrangements. Even if concession requests are not eliminated, you are more likely to get acceptance of your standard price and contract by sticking to them while maintaining a professional image than by conveying the image of a wheeler-dealer talking across the table, peddling a commodity, with the focus on price.

Good presenters can touch and change the lives of people. They can redirect the future of corporate America. They can persuade others to a course of action they want them to take. And they become too valuable to keep in their present job at their present pay. *You can be one of them.*

The steps and suggestions shown in Figures 9.4 and 9.5 will give you a winning presentation every time. For additional information on what to do and how to do it, pick up a copy of the book *Presentations Plus* by David Peoples. It's the best-sell-

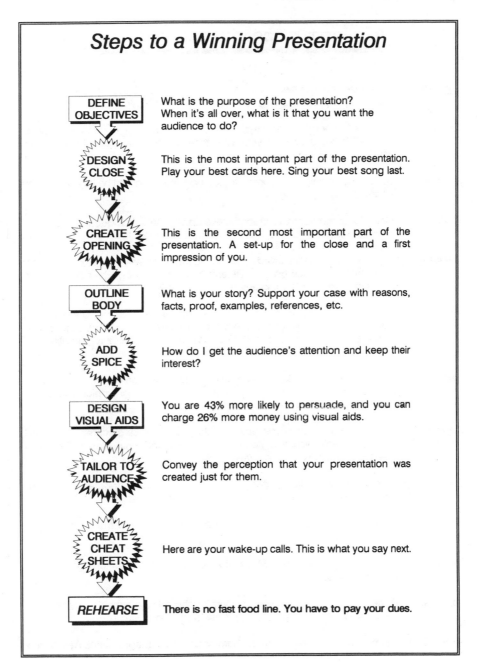

Steps to a Winning Presentation

DEFINE OBJECTIVES
What is the purpose of the presentation? When it's all over, what is it that you want the audience to do?

DESIGN CLOSE
This is the most important part of the presentation. Play your best cards here. Sing your best song last.

CREATE OPENING
This is the second most important part of the presentation. A set-up for the close and a first impression of you.

OUTLINE BODY
What is your story? Support your case with reasons, facts, proof, examples, references, etc.

ADD SPICE
How do I get the audience's attention and keep their interest?

DESIGN VISUAL AIDS
You are 43% more likely to persuade, and you can charge 26% more money using visual aids.

TAILOR TO AUDIENCE
Convey the perception that your presentation was created just for them.

CREATE CHEAT SHEETS
Here are your wake-up calls. This is what you say next.

REHEARSE
There is no fast food line. You have to pay your dues.

Figure 9.4

GETTING GOOD, GETTING BETTER

Opening   Memorize the first two minutes. Get attention and interest and create a good first impression. What are your credentials? What is the agenda?

Objective   Why are we here? When it's all over, what is it that you want them to do or believe? What action do you want them to take? Answer the question, "What's in it for them?"

Prepared   Rehearse, rehearse, rehearse. Do not read. Notes should be key words and phrases only.

Content   Good facts, numbers, references, examples, analogies, quotes, etc. Good organization, very logical, easy to follow, flows well.

Participation   Get the audience involved. Plan in advance to ask questions, ask for agreement, ask their opinion. Reference their company, their department, their job. Use their terminology, their acronyms.

Visual Aids   Simple, clear, easy to read and understand. Like a billboard. Use pictures, drawings, graphs, bar charts, pie charts. Use overlays for complex subjects. Use color. Use revelation technique. Visuals should clarify, simplify and emphasize.

Interest   Get interest and keep attention. Use questions, demonstrations, testimonials, war stories, humor (if natural), visual aids, analogies, exercises, case studies, examples, etc.

Convincing   Do you agree? Would you buy? Would you sign? Be sincere, warm, and friendly. Speak with knowledge, conviction, and enthusiasm. Establish credibility. A jury would vote yes.

Eye Contact   Do not stare at the floor, ceiling, your notes, the screen or outer space. Aim for eye contact with each person. Move around the room.

Voice   Firm, clear, sincere. Variations in pitch and pace. Avoid distractions like "uh", "ah", "o.k.,o.k.".

Movement   Do not stand in one spot. Move into the audience. Use natural gestures to add emphasis.

Appearance   Pleasant facial expression. Smile. Comfortable relaxed posture. Professional appearance. Avoid distraction of dress and mannerisms.

Strong Close   Memorize the last two minutes. Summarize. Ask for agreement. Ask for the order. Ask for action.

Figure 9.5

ing book ever written on how to develop and deliver effective presentations.

We have discussed six proven strategies to differentiate yourself from your competitors. But you don't have to pick and choose among them. You can get a double-whammy effect by putting them all together as shown in Figure 9.6.

WHAT IF YOU COULD DO IT ALL ?

- **Give a Presentation** of applying a

- **Business Philosophy** of

- **"Least Risk"**

- To a **Breakthrough Project** and

- Front-end the presentation with an
Executive Service & Support Review

- Or ask to be **1st Choice for 2nd Place**

Figure 9.6   Putting it all together.

How to Get Ahead

In all my years in selling, training, and managing, I have observed that the best marketing and selling ideas come not from headquarters but from the field—from those who are closest to the customer. I also observed that the salespeople who get ahead are not those with a silver tongue but those with golden ideas they have proved in their own territory.

Here is an opportunity for you to do for yourself and your career what we have been suggesting you do for your customers. But this time we suggest that you differentiate yourself from the other salespeople in your own company. One or more of the above ideas can be your horse to ride to not only get more business but also to get ahead.

I invite you to be proactive. For example:

- If your company doesn't have a visual presentation of your products or service, make your own. You don't have to be an artist; just be neat. And even if you paid a few bucks to a student at a local commercial art school, the return on your investment is likely to be 1,000 to 1. It's a one-time job to put together a presentation. Then you can tell your story professionally every time instead of unprofessionally many times.
- Every company has business philosophies, even though they may not be on the company stationery. If you're in doubt, just ask yourself (or your customers) why people do business with you. Then find the words to make it sound "Madison Avenue," and you're in the business of selling a philosophy.
- The fact that your company doesn't have a brochure that says "least risk" doesn't mean that you can't sell least risk. Just interpret the uniqueness of your product or service in terms of risk. I bet you can build a convincing case that you are the least-risk supplier.
- The Breakthrough Strategy is not dependent on your company's policies or programs. The key element in its success

is your questioning, your listening, and the creative adaptation of your resources to an executive want or need that is urgent and short term, with measurable results.

- You are the only person in your company who can conduct an Executive Service and Support (ESS) Review. You are the only one with the knowledge and the records who can put together a composite service and support story for your customers.
- Selling first choice for second place is 100 percent within your control in your territory. What have you got to lose?

10
Dream, Desire, & Fire
(If It Is to Be, It's up to Me)

DREAM, DESIRE, & FIRE

We have come a long way. For nine chapters I have been talking about the skills, techniques, and strategy of selling to executives. There's one additional, important ingredient—YOU. An important variable in your success is not your external skills but your internal chemistry.

- Do you have
  A dream in the head?
  A desire in the heart?
  A fire in the belly?
- Is your life a game of chance or choice?
- Do you have a passion for
  Your company?
  Your products?
  Your job?
- Are you persistent?

How you answer those questions will determine your position on the pyramid of life shown in Figure 10.1.

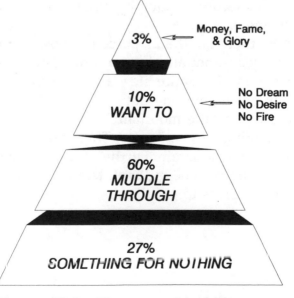

Figure 10.1 The pyramid of life.

At the top of the mountain are the superstars. They are the 3 percent who are the best there is at what they do. They live in a world of money, fame, and glory. You can be one of them.

Just below the superstars are the 10 people out of 100 who want to be at the top but are missing the key ingredients. They have no fire in the belly, no burning desire, and no goals. They are like Alice from *Alice in Wonderland*.

> "Would you tell me please, which way I ought to go from here?"
> "That depends a good deal on where you want to get to," said the cat.
> "I don't much care where," said Alice.
> "Then it doesn't much matter which way you go," said the cat.

The vast majority of salespeople comprise the 60 percent who just want to muddle through. They have low self-esteem, lack confidence, are indecisive and self-conscious, have low energy and drive, and have poor self-discipline. They would rather settle for a semi-secure mediocrity than strive toward meaningful achievement.

And finally, there are the 27 percent whose dominant characteristic is to get something for nothing. They are the order takers. They spend their entire life waiting for their ship to come in—when they never sent one out.

Where are you on the mountain?

I bring you tidings of good news. There are immediate openings at the top of the mountain. Furthermore, as shown in Figure 10.2, you do not have to be brilliant, talented, a workaholic, or have advanced degrees to get there.

Figure 10.2 You do not have to be brilliant, talented, a workaholic, or have advanced degrees to get to the top of the mountain.

You Do Not Have to Be Brilliant

The world is full of brilliant people who are poor. Consider, for example, the 55,000-plus members of Mensa (I.Q. of 135 required to get in the back door). The average member of Mensa makes less than a plumber each year.

Dr. Edward Teller, the genius of A-bomb fame, once made this statement: "A child does not need a lightning mind to be a scientist, nor does he need a miraculous memory, nor is it necessary that he get very high grades in school. The only point that counts is that the child have a high degree of interest in science." People with an I.Q. of 100 who are positive, optimistic, cooperative, and truly like what they do will earn more money and respect and achieve more success than Mensa members who are negative, pessimistic, and uncooperative.

After all, William James, the great American psychologist and philosopher, said, "We are only half awake." Scientists say that 90 percent of our capabilities lie dormant and up to 95 percent of our talents go unused.

You Do Not Have to Be Talented

As for talent—nothing is more common than unsuccessful people with talent. Most of history's greatest achievements have been accomplished not by the most talented but by people of average skill who had other, more important characteristics. Listen to the words of this man:

> No, my friend, you are quite wrong about me. I am just an ordinary individual without special ability in any line. In most things I am only just above average; in some things I am under the average rather than over. This is certainly true of my physical powers. I can't run; I'm only an ordinary walker; I'm certainly not a good swimmer. I can probably ride a horse better than I can do anything else, but I am not a remarkable horseman. Neither am I a good shot. My eyesight is so poor that I have to be near my game to take any aim at all. So you can see that, as far as physical gifts are concerned, I am just an ordinary man. The same thing is true of my literary ability. I am certainly not a brilliant writer. During my lifetime I have written a good deal, but I always have to work and slave over everything I put on paper.

So wrote the renowned military hero, explorer, lover of the outdoors, big game hunter, author, and president of the United States—Theodore Roosevelt.

You Do Not Have to Be a Workaholic

Is hard work the answer? Hardly. There are millions of people who have worked hard all their lives, yet today they are living on Social Security.

You Do Not Have to Have a Fancy Education

Do education and advanced degrees make a difference? Yes, but there is nothing so common as a well-educated person. The world is full of educated derelicts. And did you know that 15 percent of all millionaires did not finish high school?

Here are twelve famous lawyers. *Which one was a law school drop-out?*

- Patrick Henry . . . Governor of Virginia
- John Jay . . . Chief Justice, U.S. Supreme Court
- John Marshall . . . Chief Justice, U.S. Supreme Court
- William Wirt . . . U.S. Attorney General
- Roger Taney . . . Chief Justice, U.S. Supreme Court
- Daniel Webster . . . Secretary of State
- Salmon Chase . . . Chief Justice, U.S. Supreme Court
- Abraham Lincoln .. President of U.S.
- Stephen Douglas . . . U.S. Senator
- Clarence Darrow .. World Famous Lawyer
- Robert Storey . . . President, American Bar Association
- Strom Thurmond . . . U.S. Senator

Only one was a law school dropout. He was Clarence Darrow. The other 11 did not drop out of law school, *because they never went to law school at all.*

Let me summarize for you 20 years of study by Dr. Charles Garfield as documented in 318 pages of his book *Peak Performers*. He concludes that peak performers are

- Not born but made.
- Not superhuman with special talents, but average people like you and me.
- Not workaholics, but committed to results instead of activities.

And so indeed there are extraordinary possibilities in ordinary people. As Satchel Paige of baseball fame put it, "Nobody can help being born common, but ain't nobody got to remain ordinary."

We have a choice. We need not spend our lives wallowing in misery, insecurity, and mediocrity.

And so today I invite you to catch the tide—it's at its flood.

Answer the knock—it's at your door. It may not pass this way again. The walk along the Road to Glory starts today. You can be the captain of your ship and the master of your fate. You can be one of the 3 percent.

Throughout recorded history, people have looked for common denominators among leaders, winners, and achievers. They are not easy to find. One commonality shared by all great men and women throughout history has been a vivid picture of themselves in the future having already achieved their goal. They have a dream in the head.

They have an intense commitment to what they do and what they want. High achievers call it by different names—a passion, a mission, a purpose, a deep feeling, or a fire in the belly. They credit their success more clearly to that passion than to aptitude—more to desire than to knowledge or education.

Oliver Wendell Holmes was talking about them when he said, "Every calling is great when greatly pursued."

On the other side of the coin are those who are well educated with natural talent but have no passion, no purpose, and no commitment.

Most people aim at nothing and hit it with amazing accuracy.

The need for meaning and purpose in life is one of the great drives in human nature. We are built to solve problems, conquer obstacles, and achieve goals. Those who have none wander in circles. They find life aimless and boring and are plagued with depression. They are missing the spark of life.

One of the miracles of the mind is its ability to rationalize almost anything. Unsuccessful people, without exception, have reasons to explain their lack of achievement. Repeated often enough, they come to believe and feel comfortable with their excuses, which in time become self-fulfilling prophecies. The great philosophers describe the results this way:

We first make our habits, and then our habits make us.

—John Dryden

Habit is a cable. We weave a thread of it every day, and at last we cannot break it.

—Horace Mann

The chains of habit are generally too small to be felt until they are too strong to be broken.

—Samuel Johnson

Habit, if not resisted, soon becomes necessity.

—St. Augustine

The most common excuses can be summarized in what I call the "If Only" game. They sound like this:

IF ONLY
I was younger.
I was older.
I had more money.
I had a better education.
I was more talented.
I had more experience.
I had a good mate.
I was free.

I wasn't so shy.
I wasn't overweight.
I wasn't underweight.
I didn't have so many problems.

If none of the above fit, then there's always the great catch-all: "If only other people understood me."

The common denominator of all these "if onlys" is a comparison of ourselves to others. Although that tendency may be overwhelming, the fact is that the characteristics of others are irrelevant to your success. It is not against them that you compete.

"I have found the enemy and he is me."

If you doubt this truth, come step into my parlor. I want you to meet some people.

- This man is blind.
- This one is deaf.
- That man was tongue-tied at birth.
- Here is a black woman born 20th of 22 children. She was a sick child and wore leg braces for six years.

The blind man wrote *Paradise Lost*. His name is John Milton.
The one who is deaf you know by his music—Beethoven.
The greatest orator in the history of Greece, Demosthenes, was tongue-tied at birth.
And the first American woman to win three gold medals at the Olympics was Wilma Rudolph.

Who would have believed that a one-armed man would become a professional baseball player? that a man with no feet would run a marathon? that it's possible to be an artist and have no arms? that a man with half a foot would kick a 63-yard field goal and be elected to the Football Hall of Fame? Or that the man who may have the greatest living brain since Einstein is confined to a wheelchair and cannot speak—though Stephen Hawking wrote a best seller (*A Brief History of Time*) and lectures all over the world through an interpreter.

A study of over 400 prominent people revealed that 75 percent of them had been handicapped by tragedy, disabilities, or great frustration. The lives of great people throughout history prove that being crippled, uneducated, blind, or poor are not barriers to success—or even greatness. It is not just one or two but thousands who have walked from the ghetto into greatness.

An even greater delusion than the "if only" game is to not even play in the game. This cop-out is based on the belief that our futures are determined by luck and fate—by a roll of the dice, by the signs of the zodiac, or by biorhythms and sunspots. Sometimes people say things like this: "What ever will be, will be." This is a state of mind based on the premise that we have no control over our destinies. These people see themselves as pawns on some giant chess board of the universe. They hope for a day when lightning will strike and they will be chosen to receive the bounty that others possess. They see themselves as either victims of the system or as one of the chosen few—when in fact they are volunteers who are cooperating in their own failure. Not surprisingly, they are the lotteries' main customers.

Life Is Not a Game of Chance—
Life Is a Game of Choice

Oliver Wendell Holmes said, "We need education in the obvious rather than investigation in the obscure." In opposition to the fiction of luck is the law of cause and effect, which states that for every effect in our lives there is a specific cause. Because we have the ability to change the causes, we can change the effects. If we wish our lives to be different in the future, we have to change the causes in the present. The seed you sow will be the lawn you mow. Life doesn't care who succeeds and who fails— it's up to you. Success is not a pie with only so many slices to go around. The law of cause and effect will prevail. So-called luck is what happens when preparation meets opportunity. Success comes not from being dealt a good hand but in playing well the cards you have. Most of history's greatest achievements were not made by people who were dealt a royal flush but by those with a pair of jacks.

We Control the Dice of Life

There are six major areas of your life that you control. These are the causes. What you do and how you do in these six areas, depicted in Figure 10.3, will determine the degree of sunshine in your future.

You Control the Clock

We can't stop the clock, but we can control how we use our time. All of us have the same amount, but one of the biggest differences between the 3 percent and the others is how they use their time.

You Choose Your Own Friends

We control whom we choose to spend our time with. Do we choose positive, inspiring role models who have something we want or negative and depressed people who are preoccupied with criticizing places, people, and things? We tend to take on the characteristics of those with whom we associate.

If you want to catch the flu, just hang around with people who have it. If you want to become a tramp—hang out with tramps. If you want to become a failure, then choose other failures for your friends. If you want to succeed, then spend your time with successful people.

So choose well. Stay away from the bottom of the pyramid. Don't be one of the flock. Eagles don't fly in flocks—you have to find them one at a time.

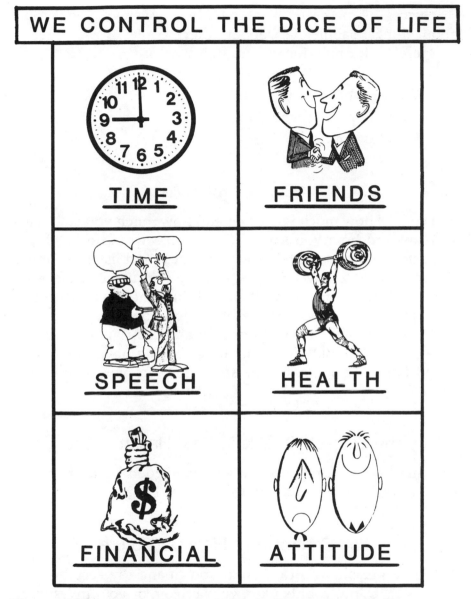

Figure 10.3   How are you doing in these areas that you control?

Successful people talk about ideas. Average people talk about things. Failures talk about other people.

Here's a formula for success that works:

- Decide what you want to do
- Find the person who does it best
- Do what he or she does

You Control Your Mouth

You control how much you listen and how much you talk, what you say and how you say it. The people who are liked and respected the most are those who talk less and listen the most. We don't have to have an opinion on every subject. In fact, for most subjects we are not well enough informed to have a credible opinion. We would do well to follow the wisdom of "Desiderata": "Speak your truth quietly and clearly; and listen to others, even the dull and ignorant; they too have their story. Avoid loud and aggressive persons, they are vexations to the spirit."

The Biggest Variable in Your Health Is You

The question is simply this: Do you have good health habits or bad health habits? You know the answer better than anyone.

You Control Your Financial Future

The only person who can make you financially secure—even rich—is YOU, not your banker, your broker, or your investment advisor. Just as war is too important to be left to the generals, so your financial future is too important to be left to the experts. Do not learn this lesson the hard way, as John F. Kennedy did after the Bay of Pigs fiasco when he said, "How could I have been so mistaken as to have trusted the experts?"

You Control Your Attitude

William James once said, "The greatest discovery of my generation is that men can alter their lives by changing their thinking." Do you live in a world of gloom, doom, and rain or one of good, glory, and sunshine? The mind is like a light switch. Your world can be light and bright or dark and dreary. The switch is in your hand.

If It Is to Be, It's up to Me

We can, we should, and we must accept the responsibility for our own destinies. Our future lies not in the stars but within ourselves, to paraphrase Shakespeare. The "man upstairs" is not our navigator. He gave each of us the intellect and the wherewithal to chart our own course—to write our own books. We have a choice. We are the only ones who can use the talent we have.

"Qué Será, Será" was a charming love song of days gone by. Unfortunately it is a myth—no, a lie. Those who hang their hat on this philosophy of life will self-destruct their own potential. They rust out rather than wear out.

There are three differences between us and all other creatures on the planet:

1. We possess the gift of laughter.
2. We are aware that someday we will not be here—we will die.
3. We are able to change the future. We have choices.

The benefits of taking control of our lives are enormous. A study at the University of California at Berkeley revealed that the happiest and best-adjusted people are those who believe they have a high degree of control over their lives. They also responded better to unfolding events and handled change with less apprehension. They learn from their mistakes rather than replay them, and they spend their time working in the present rather than fearing the future.

Judith Rodin, a Yale University psychologist, says feelings of control and self-determination are "of central importance in influencing psychological and physical health, and perhaps even longevity." Which profession would you think boasts the greatest average longevity of its members? The answer is symphony conductors. It is said that they, of all professionals, have the greatest control over what they do and how they do it.

Indecisiveness and procrastination are the chosen ways of life for most people. They follow the course of least resistance, which is to do nothing. This provides a security blanket of

- Never being wrong
- Never making mistakes
- Never being disappointed
- Never failing

But they will also never succeed.

Of all the words of tongue or pen, the saddest are these: "What might have been." Or, to quote H. G. Wells, "The only true measure of success is the ratio between what we might have been and what we became."

David Livingstone, the great explorer, said, "I will go anywhere so long as it is forward." Confucius taught, "He who tries something and fails is infinitely greater than he who tries nothing and succeeds." And Henry Wadsworth Longfellow wrote

Let the lives of great men all remind us
We can make our lives sublime.
And in parting leave behind us
Footprints in the sands of time.

Persistence

A characteristic of winners is great persistence. Or, as they say down in the valley, a big shot is nothing more than a little shot who kept shooting. In China they would quote Confucius, who said, "It does not matter how slowly you go, so long as you do not stop."

The course of least resistance is to give up if you lose the first round. We forget that the first round is just that—the first round. A temporary defeat is not a permanent failure. There is not a winner alive who has not experienced temporary defeat. Remember, success is never final, and failure is never fatal.

Consider the following statistics of salespeople:

44% give up after one "No"
22% give up after two "Nos"
14% give up after three "Nos"
12% give up after four "Nos"
92%

In summary, 92 percent of all salespeople give up after no sales on the fourth call. Yet 60 percent of all customers say no four times before saying yes.

In fact, you should remember from Chapter 6 that it takes an average of five to seven calls to sell to an Analytical and four to five to sell to an Amiable. And those two groups make up 70 percent of the prospects.

A president of the United States said it best: "Nothing in the world can take the place of persistence. Talent will not. Nothing is more common than unsuccessful men with talent. Genius will not. Unrewarded genius is almost a proverb. Education will not. The world is full of educated derelicts. Persistence, determination and hard work makes the difference." So said Calvin Coolidge.

One of the most dramatic examples of perseverance in the face of repeated defeats is the professional record of this man:

- Failed in business in '31
- Elected to the legislature in '32
- Failed again in business in '34

- His girlfriend died in '35
- He suffered a nervous breakdown in '36
- He was defeated for Speaker in '38
- Defeated for Congress in '43
- Elected to Congress in '46
- Defeated for Congress in '48
- Defeated for Senate in '55
- Defeated for vice-president in '56
- Defeated again for the Senate in '58

But two years later in 1860, Abraham Lincoln was elected president of the United States.

If you need more proof of the value of persistence, just listen to this unbelievable story of failure.

- At age 14 he dropped out of school
- Became a farm hand . . . hated it
- Was a streetcar conductor . . . hated it
- Joined the army . . . hated it
- Tried blacksmithing . . . failed
- Became a railroad locomotive fireman . . . was fired
- Studied law . . . dropped out
- Sold insurance . . . failed
- Sold tires . . . failed
- Ran a ferryboat . . . quit
- Ran a gas station . . . failed
- Finally, late in life, he became a cook and bottle washer at a restaurant in Corbin, Kentucky—and did all right until a new highway bypassed the restaurant.

Time had run out—he was an old man. His first Social Security check had arrived. But this man took that check and started a new business. His name was Colonel Harland Sanders, and his business was called Kentucky Fried Chicken.

Are You on the Right Road?

The first thing to remember is that no person—absolutely no one—has final authority over your destiny but you. You may honor or respect a parent or a close friend, but the closest friend you will ever have is yourself. You must be a friend to yourself first. You must be a success with yourself before you can be a success with others.

—Maxwell Maltz

Is this the road you want to travel, or should you have taken the other fork? A mandatory requirement for true success and happiness is to truly enjoy what you do. When you are doing work you love, you can truly say, "I never worked a day in my life."

Many people acquire the outward symbols of success. But 20 years later when they go to open their treasure chest to enjoy the fruits of their labor, they find it empty. They failed to realize that the joy is in the journey, not the destination. After 20 years of climbing the ladder to get to the top, they find it is leaning against the wrong wall. They missed the spice of life. Malcolm Forbes said it best: "If you don't enjoy the climb, giving what it takes to get to the top isn't worth it."

We have different talents and abilities. Some have many—some have few. But every human being has the ability to excel or make an outstanding contribution in at least one area. And that is all we need. Success is doing what you are good at and what you enjoy. Everything we could ever hope for is either in our heads, our hands, or under our feet.

It is a great sadness to discover that after many years of struggle the object of your effort will not bring happiness. Sadder still is the conclusion that it is too late to turn back and start over. Most people will continue to the end of an unhappy trail. They made a poor choice early in life and have compounded the error through the years. Or as frequently happens, we allow the choice to be made for us—by a well-meaning family or by circumstances.

A survey of 1350 people by the Gallup Organization revealed that only 41 percent of those responding held jobs they had planned. Sixty-five percent said that given a second chance to start over, they would get more information about career options. Another study revealed that 62 percent of all employees fell into their present positions by accident. I ask you, where is it written that you have to keep doing what you're doing? Consider, for example, these words of wisdom: "I am not in this world to live up to your expectations." You have the right to

- Set your own priorities
- Choose your own lifestyle
- Make an honest mistake
- Change your mind

Remember this:

When what you do is what you want
And what you want is what you believe
      then
Your productivity is the greatest
Your self-esteem is the highest
Your happiness is the fullest.

Ayn Rand, author of *Atlas Shrugged* and *The Fountainhead,* said, "No one's happiness but my own is in my power to achieve or destroy."

We need to ask ourselves this question: What would we do with our lives if money was not a factor?

On one end of the spectrum, let us consider Mahatma Gandhi who said, "There is more to life than increasing its speed." He lived in a hut with a dirt floor, no phone, and no electricity. When he died, his total worldly possessions consisted of a pair of sandals, a robe, and a pair of glasses. But as the unquestioned leader of 500 million people and as the role model for future leaders who also changed the course of history, Gandhi is immortal and will live throughout recorded history.

The results of choosing without regard for money can be surprising. For example, in a study of 1500 people, 83 percent chose careers for the money and only 17 percent chose based solely on what they loved to do. Twenty years later there were 103 millionaires. All but 2 of them came from the 17 percent.

The fact is that 65 percent of the workforce doesn't like what they do. Yet the simple truth is you will be happier and perform better in a job you like versus one you dislike.

Linus Pauling said that he received a Nobel Prize for "having fun." Jacques Cousteau says that he has spent his life "playing." The immortal Bear Bryant said, "Coaching is my hobby." And the great philosopher and thinker Joseph Campbell advised us all to "follow our bliss." Whatever you're ready for is ready for you. Let us not be deceived by these two great myths:

Myth #1: I'm sure I can do and be happy in any job. What really counts is the title and pay level.

Myth #2: Management and only management equals success.

Do You Have a Passion?

Only the persuaded can persuade.

Do you have a passion for your company, your products or service, and your job? Are you committed? If there is hesitancy in your answer, your customers can give you what you need.

Go to your six best customers and ask them why they chose your company, your products, and you. Write down what they say, then reread it before your next sales call and start acting and talking like a satisfied customer. If you act enthusiastically, you will become enthusiastic. And enthusiasm is the highest-paid quality on earth. It is a fact that nothing happens until someone gets excited. People are persuaded more by the depth of your conviction than the height of your logic, more by your enthusiasm than any proof you can offer. Listen to the wisdom of Goethe and begin it now.

Begin It Now

Until one is committed, there is hesitancy,
the chance to draw back, always ineffectiveness.

Concerning all acts of initiative (and creation),
there is one elementary truth, the ignorance of which
kills countless ideas and splendid plans.

That the moment one definitely commits oneself,
then Providence moves too.

All sorts of things occur to help one
that would never otherwise have occurred.

A whole stream of events issues from the decision,
raising in one's favor all manner of unforeseen incidents
and meetings and material assistance, which no man
could have dreamed would have come his way.

Whatever you can do, or dream you can, begin it.

Boldness has Genius, Power, and Magic in it.

Begin it now.

Goethe

Epilogue

I walk the beach (the tide is low) and ponder my love affair with Big Blue. What a wonderful journey it was. How lucky I have been. How proud I was to wear the blue suit, the white shirt, the ten-pound shoes with a thousand eyes and say, "I work for IBM." Even today, my vision is still blurred as I see only through the lens of the culture that was IBM. I am "the desire for excellence, respect for the individual, and the best customer service in the world." Big Blue is in my blood.

But the winds of change are in the air. The storm clouds grow dark. The old ways no longer work. The business has changed. There are new players with new toys and new ways.

Is my beloved IBM destined to become an ordinary company? Or worse, is there to be a day when the sun fails to rise on the international giant on which it never set?

I am saddened as the eye of the storm approaches on this ocean of change. I look at IBM, and I think of Odysseus in the story told by Homer:

Darkness swooped down from the sky. East Wind and South and the tempestuous West fell to on one another, and from the North came a white squall, rolling a great wave in its van. Odysseus' knees shook and his spirit quailed. In anguish he communed with that great heart of his: "Poor wretch, what will your end be now? I fear the goddess prophesied all too well when she told me I should have my full measure of agony on the sea before I reached my native land. Every word she said is coming true, as I can tell by the sky, with its vast coronet of clouds from Zeus, and by the sea that he has raised with angry squalls from every quarter."

As he spoke, a mountainous wave, advancing with majestic sweep, crashed down upon him from above and whirled his vessel round. The steering-oar was torn from his hands, and he himself was tossed off the boat, while at the same moment the warring winds joined forces in one tremendous gust, which snapped the mast in two and flung the sail and yard far out into the sea. For a long time Odysseus was kept under water. Weighed down by the clothes which the goddess Calypso had given him, he found it no easy matter to fight his way up against the downrush of that mighty wave. But at last he reached the air and spat out the bitter brine that kept streaming down his face.

Will IBM, like Odysseus, survive the storm? Will the days of glory come again? I walk the beach (the tide is high) and ponder a vision of the future.

There is a tide

In the affairs of men,

Which, taken at the flood

Leads on to fortune;

Omitted, all the voyage

of their life

Is bound in shallows

and in miseries.

-- *Shakespeare*

Index

Focused strategies, 54, 55
Forbes, Malcolm, 219
Ford, Gerald, 98
Forecasting, sales
  and walk-away selling
    strategies, 56–57
The Fountainhead (Rand), 220
Freud, Sigmund, 169
Friends, 212–14
FUD factor, 186

G

Gandhi, Mahatma, 220
Garfield, Charles, 208
Gas companies as potential
  customers, 77–79
Gatekeepers
  characteristics of, 31–32
  and customers' buying
    decisions, 48, 50
  and dominant influencers, 40
Girard, Joe, 170
Goethe, Johann Wolfgang von,
  221–22
Greenberg, Herbert, 101
Growth and customers' buying
  decisions, 43–47
Guinness Book of World Records,
  170

H

Hawking, Stephen, 211
Health, 214
Heiman, Stephen, 25, 43
Henry, Patrick, 207
Holmes, Oliver Wendell, 208, 211
Homer, 224
*How to Win Friends and Influence
  People* (Carnegie), 171
Hughes, Charles Evans, 148
Human priorities, 11–12

I

Iacocca, Lee, 98
IBM
  and changing market forces,
    224–25
  customer critiques of, 127
  customer satisfaction at, 160
  executive calls at, 83
  and key indicator information
    strategies, 119
  product quality at, 165
  salesforce of, 2–4, 63, 72
  selling strategies at, 18
Indirect people, 89–90
Influencers
  characteristics of, 28, 30–31
  and customers' buying
    decisions, 48, 50
  and dominant influencers, 40

J

James, William, 169, 206, 215
Jay, John, 207
Johnson, Samuel, 209
Johnson, Wesley J., 25
Jung, Carl, 85

K

Kennedy, John F., 214

L

Land, Vickey, 170
Least-risk strategy, 185–86,
  199–200
Levitt, Ted, 14
Libraries and knowledge of
  customers, 73, 75, 76, 80
Lincoln, Abraham, 207, 218
Listening, 214
  in selling, 127–34, 171